Showers and Bright Spells
Selected Poems 2009-2019

Henri Droguet

*Translated from the French by
Alexander Dickow*

SPUYTEN DUYVIL
New York City

© 2021 Henri Droguet
translation © 2021 Alexander Dickow
ISBN 978-1-956005-01-1

Library of Congress Cataloging-in-Publication Data

Names: Droguet, Henri, author. | Dickow, Alexander, translator. | Droguet, Henri. Averses et sorts lumineux. | Droguet, Henri. Averses et sorts lumineux. English.
Title: Showers and bright spells : selected poems 2009-2019 / Henri Droguet ; translated from the French by Alexander Dickow.
Description: New York City : Spuyten Duyvil, [2021] | Title of original work: Averses et sorts lumineux. | Parallel text in French and English.
Identifiers: LCCN 2021036093 | ISBN 9781956005011 (paperback)
Subjects: LCSH: Droguet, Henri--Translations into English. | LCGFT: Poetry.
Classification: LCC PQ2664.R53 A9413 2021 | DDC 841/.914--dc23
LC record available at https://lccn.loc.gov/2021036093

Contents

A Translator's Introduction

Clatters

    Literally / Littéralement 2

    Romance (suite) / Romance (suite) 4

    Yarnspun / À dormir debout 8

    Uncertain Invention of Chasms / Incertaine invention des gouffres 10

    Against a Dark Field / À contre-nuit 12

    Passage into Darkness / Passage à l'obscur 14

    Congé / Congé 16

    Moderate Gale Warning / Avis de grand frais 18

    Other Gardens / Autres jardins 22

    Clatters / Boucans 24

Bonus Poems published with *Clatters*

    Offshore (note) / Au large (note) 28

    Soliloquy / Soliloque 30

    I, I, I / Je je je 32

    Shoot Again (Final Ball) / Re-jeu (pour en finir) 34

Palimpsests & Rigaudons

    Tohu-bohu / Tohu-bohu 38

    Chimera / Chimère 40

    Fixed Point 2 / Point fixe 2 42

    The Announcement / L'annoncement 44

    Vademecum / Vademecum 46

    Once and for All / Une fois pour toutes 48

    Imprecation / Imprécation 50

    Pot-pourri / Pot-pourri 52

Declensions / Déclinaisons 56

Frolic / Folâtrerie 58

Rusticities / Rusticités 60

Before Going Out / Avant la sortie 62

On the Way / En route 64

Real Label on a Simulated Bottle / Étiquette vraie sur une bouteille feinte 68

A Life / Une vie 70

Factory / Manufacture 72

To Name Names / Noms de noms 74

Fable of Contents / Fable des matières 78

Sketches In My Red Zap Book

Quatuor no. 3 82

Text Message / Texto 84

In the Ancient Manner / À l'ancienne 88

Update / Mise à jour 90

Artist's Trial / Épreuve d'artiste 94

Brief / Bref 98

Ritornello / Ritournelle 100

Snapshot / Cliché 102

Machinery 2 / Machinerie 2 104

Orpheus / Orphée 112

Figure / Figure 116

I Haven't Said My Final Word / Je n'ai pas dit mon dernier mot 118

Precipitations

Rain Steam and Speed / Pluie vent vitesse 122

Bulletin (supplement) / Bulletin (supplément) 124

Continuation / Continuation 126

Nothing (a Whole Lot Of) / Rien (trois fois) 130

Frivolities / Frivolités 134

The Depths of Time / Le Fonds des temps 138

Destocking / Déstockage 142

Ancient History 1 / Histoire ancienne 1 146

Ancient History 2 / Histoire ancienne 2 148

Sketch / Esquisse 150

Memorandum / Pour mémoire 152

Juxtapositions / Juxtapositions 154

Oompahs / Flonflons 156

Twilight / Crépuscule 158

Discharge / Quitus 160

Chivaree, certified true copy / Charivari, p.c.c. 164

Good and Grand / Grand beau 168

Parade / Parade 172

Down Time / Temps mort 174

Impromptu / Impromptu 178

Acknowledgments 181

SHOWERS AND BRIGHT SPELLS

A Translator's Introduction
—Droguet's "Unkempt Opera"

In the twenty years since I first encountered Henri Droguet's work, I've attempted a good many times by now to give some account of it, and a little of the man who makes it. But it's hard to account for the sea, relentlessly itself in the inexhaustible nuances of its weather. I've tried on occasion to situate Droguet's work in the broader landscape of contemporary French poetry; to locate his "position," to borrow Bourdieu's term—I notably lent myself to that task in my afterword to *Clatters*, a chapbook which has since become a part of the present volume. Now, situating Droguet is a difficult enough task. But to speak about the poems without merely repeating them, to speak *through* them without speaking *for* them, that is something else again. Consider the present attempt the fruit of many years' observation and translation, as far as it goes.

I began just now with the sea.

As proper as it would seem to call this poetry "oceanic," the word smacks too much of Hugo and Tennyson and their grandiloquence, whereas this word ought to convey something considerably more obscure, more obstinate and less human than the *merely* grand or vast—something elemental and meteorological, for example. For the oceanic also involves the monotonous, age-long grinding of the water against stone (does every wave leave its imperceptible mark, until the stone has at last been made smooth?), a kind of painstaking, indefatigable industry; it involves garbage retched up onto the shore, and the stench of ancient slime. It is vast, but it intimates its incomprehensible immensity by way of the trivial and the small, like the dim figure at the center of Caspar David Friedrich's "Monk by the sea" (but Droguet, a regular practitioner of sailing himself, may be a good deal more worldly than the monk).

Friedrich was, of course, a quintessentially romantic painter, and so Droguet is himself a romantic of sorts, a distant inheritor of the Hugos and Tennysons—or, much more appropriately, of the Heines and the Blakes. But he is so in the dissonant, ostensibly anti-romantic mode of Tristan Corbière, one of his most important literary forebears, whose caustic and often self-deprecating humor derives from tonal dissonance (the French call this *humour grinçant*, rasping or creaky humor, humor that makes noise). As in Corbière's work (Corbière is also obsessed with the ocean), there is in Droguet no genius contemplating the mirror-image of his inner order in the harmony of the natural landscape. Instead, there's a rather tiny and grotesque little *person* considering that landscape—with amazement of course, but also with some degree of terror: the harmony, inner and outer, is hardly to be found; at best, the little figure might find the wherewithal to laugh a bit (creakily), or to sing a little song:

> *jabbering fidgeting*
> *the lyre and all the tralala*
> *boom boom with feeling*
> *ah just make us laugh* ("Nothing (a Whole Lot Of)")

This little man, this somewhat risible, terribly familiar figure shivering in the corner of our worldcanvas, may be as old as time, and has been described in the following terms by the French poet Claude Roy, in reference to Droguet's work:

> And in a quite modest corner of the giant malouinoscopic[1] landscape, a tiny little fellow, a stunned flea, sarcastic, querulous, astonished. Hands in his pockets, he looks at that great expanse of water, of heath, of gusts, that universe ready to gobble him up in one bite. And he asks, Droguet does (the ocean? God? who?): "Can you tell me what I'm doing here?" But the wind blows so powerfully that the answer is lost in the natural ruckus of nature.[2]

---

1 Malouinoscopic, i.e. from the point of view of the Malouin, an inhabitant of the city of Saint-Malo, which Droguet has been for a very long time (NdT).
2 Claude Roy, review of *Chant rapace*, *Cahier de Poésie*, no. 3, October 1980, my translation.

I mentioned that this little man might be described as "grotesque," but that's only as long as the original strict sense of the term is maintained (once again, in France, by way of Hugo, as well as Théophile Gautier and others). The grotesque is, above all, a *mixture*, of beauty and ugliness, order and disorder; it is a jumble of contrasts, disjointed. Droguet's poetry, like the world, fits this description. He has quoted Paul Claudel's remark to me: "disorder is the delight of the imagination."

Because of this dissonance, it's tempting to overstate the negative dimension of Droguet's work, yet an excess of the negative may burst at any moment into affirmation, devastation into celebration, lament into hymn—and back again nearly as abruptly. Take this glimpse of idyll from "Good and Grand":

> imminent
> bursting out in the unrincing yaw
> of shadow and the retreat
> of a cloud chipped unstitched
> floats the semblance of a black
> smile whose grace all of a sudden
> boisters
>   then more
>   or less is erased

All the way up to and including the word "black," the tone is ominous, as of something terrible approaching; the cloud is "chipped" and "unstitched," battered and in danger of disintegration — but with the word "smile," the poem swerves into a clearing, though it be brief indeed in the uncertainty of things. Droguet's poetry is as fickle as the weather, and not occasionally paradoxical, seeming cheered and disheartened all at once. Blame and praise are tangled together; moments that seem pure happen by...and pass. Bleakhymns or blithepsalms—something like that, in imitation of

Paul Celan, seems in order, reaching for some term that might reflect Droguet's concoction of feelings.

The jumbled character of the existent in these poems does not preclude organic unity: they have clear beginnings and endings, and something of an arc to their development. "Quatuor no. 3" begins "All in chaos," announcing the clutter of descriptors that follow:

> crumbled
> cankered boiled coppery
> scaly sill tossle
> of opal silks and mauve
> cleft of gold goateed feathery
> purlings and darnings

The enumeration seems to come unmoored from any representational logic: what's being described is just the "chaos" announced in the poem's first line; we don't know what's being "described" or evoked until line seven, which declares, "that's all the sky is," followed by more evocations of the sky's visual qualities:

> chaos of mud blender
> polychromatic ice creamery where the grey
> the slate blue horizon the honeyed
> plumbing-gold steep trickle
> the shadows' luminous refrigerations
> and Betelgeuse blushing unto death

The poet resembles a painter smearing various colors against the canvas; the poem recalls Constable or the less well-known Eugène Boudin, both painters of the infinite variations of the heavens, and both among Droguet's favorite painters (Baudelaire's Salon of 1859 also sings the praises of Boudin's work). The sky is "grey," no, it is "slate blue" to "honeyed" or "plumbing-gold," all this from the earlier "coppery," "opal silks" and "mauve / cleft of gold"—the colors shift, refusing ever to stabilize into a clear representation ("polychromatic" evidently plays the role of a keyword in this sequence). Indeed, the poet often reiterates his opposition to straightforward representation, as on the programmatic back cover of a recent collection, *Maintenant ou jamais* (Now or Never): "I don't write figurative poetry. Pierre Soulages says: 'I don't represent, I present.' Well, there you have it, I don't figure, I disfigure, and it's an elemental, verbal tohu-bohu that I throw into space, into music, into crisis, into disorder..."[3]

But we were exploring order, not disorder, in "Quatuor no. 3." The poem's conclusion takes the reader beyond the multifarious clouds, to red Betelgeuse glinting, itself dying, and this change in perspective—the vast heavens become small and ephemeral relative to the star's ancient distance—provides the poem with a fitting conclusion that recalls Pascal's sublime astonishment before the infinitely small and the infinitely vast. "All in chaos...that's all the sky is...and Betelgeuse [...]" provides a structure, a skeleton to the poem, a beginning/middle/end within which the poet's freewheeling improvisations unfold.

In short, order and disorder blend and intertwine in Droguet's poetry. Enumerations tend to embed themselves in further enumerations, creating the impression of innumerable layers, or verbal waves crashing upon smaller waves. The sentence in "Quatuor no. 3" beginning "chaos of mud" has a sentence structure, but each element tends to fold and redivide into several elements, forming a series of smaller enumerations or verbal stutterings. Droguet offers "the grey / the slate blue horizon"; the adjective is doubled. The shadows' "luminous refrigerations" "steep trickle"; the verb is doubled (and plural—it seems to refer to "the...horizon the honeyed plumbing gold" as a plural subject). In the relative clause "where the grey...", the horizon is doubled into "the...horizon the honeyed plumbing-gold," and so forth. A single, stable term is rarely offered; instead, each element of the sentence tends to proliferate into sev-

---

3 Back cover of *Maintenant ou jamais*, Belin, 2013, my translation.

eral. The two final lines, however, cannot be integrated into the overall sentence structure: the last two lines concerning Betelgeuse are a nominal phrase, verbless, hovering there like the red giant itself far above the clouds.

In the French, these redoublings and enumerations and juxtapositions tend to follow recurrent phonological patterns; Droguet tends to favor certain endings (-*ouille* and -*aille*, -*asse*, -*ard*, -*ure*), many of which generally have depreciative connotations, or the prefixes *re-* and *dé-* (not coincidentally the prefixes of repetition and of undoing). The sounds *gn-* and *cr-* recur frequently as well. Many of these do not translate with quite the resonance of the original, although in "Quatuor no. 3" one finds the same prevalence of *-y* (feathery, coppery, etc.) as of *-eux/-euse* in the French. These patterns establish what I once called the *crunchiness* of Droguet's language, its sonic and seemingly edible sensuality. But the French might also find something faintly vulgar in some of these patterns, an echo of something grimy (*crasseux*) at work in the cosmos, a reminder of the universal mess. "Yarnspun" coins an evocative neologism for this, "encrugé" ("encrudged").

Yet in the mud one strikes upon the occasional jewel:

> and it came to an end   it was
> the digging   it was
> unknowing tenderness

This too is from "Yarnspun", which features werewolves throwing turds and other detritus, and yet this "unknowing tenderness"—of eternal sleep, perhaps (what is the digging for, if not for the grave), or of those fairytales evoked in the poem's title, or of something else again—strikes an unexpected high-lyrical note, of sweet respite. Rugged appearances notwithstanding, Droguet is a poet capable of great lightness, particularly in the poems' terminal cadences, where the turmoil comes momentarily to a rest. Some of his poems are storms that end as lullabies.

If I keep returning to this device of sudden reversal ("ah! spew! christening!"—the soiled become the baptized), it is because Droguet belongs to that choice literary breed called the ironist. This species abounds in the French tradition, perhaps much more than in our more earnest American culture. Voltaire is, of course, its most emblematic practitioner, but the problem with irony has always been that it subsumes so many varieties under the illusion of a singular label: Droguet bears more resemblance to Rabelais or the tender Sterne than to Voltaire's wit; there is little frank sarcasm here. While Voltaire's irony is perched high up along the sneering ridge of self-assurance, Droguet is suspicious of all elevated positions, even those to which he shows himself to be drawn. The sublimity of the ocean and the heavens, are Droguet's temptations: the lyrical ascensions these suppose are often undercut, sometimes before they are allowed to begin. "it is the tranquil hour when copiously / a cow pisses in the fog" ("Rusticities"). The "tranquil hour" hints at the kind of idyllic rural scene one might find in Apollinaire's "Autumn," for instance, but that idyll is cut short by the excremental animal, reality bursting uncomfortably into the lyrical dream. Although for Droguet, raised in Cherbourg, Normandy, the pissing cow may be nothing more than a perfectly natural occurrence, it does puncture the idyllic quality of these lines, with humor if not with disgust.

Droguet's work is full of such tonal ruptures, of registers derailed, and unexpected swerves, and these often occur after lyrical moments (moments of temptation!):

>   downpours and lulls
>   the crazy proverbs
>   the lovely girls strolling and the happy gallants
>   have you seen do think on it
>   the phaneroptera
>   the ephippiger and the oedipoda?
>   ("Real Label on a Simulated Bottle")

Here, the scientific names of insect species interfere with the carefree vision of "lovely girls" and "happy gallants," and while these insects may be signs of spring or summer and teeming life, they still clash with the established melody. Droguet would hardly be Droguet without his constant and salutary humor (including the occasional pun), a device of his skepticism, because it deflates self-serious posturing, the strutting of the poet in his comfortable laurels. There is a lucidity and a humility in this humor that befits our cosmic insignificance:

>   embarking
> yonder to
>   shut up
>   **COME ON YOU MUMUSES!**
>   knowing at long last
>   this modest and complicated art
>   of firmly holding your tongue
>   to stay alive
>   ("Ancient History I")

All grandiose inspiration is rejected through the figure of the ridiculed (mu)muses. Paradoxically, the poet seems here to compare his own art to that of *not* speaking, of "holding your tongue" in order "to stay alive" (although "holding one's tongue" is also maintaining control over poetry's turbulent ship.) The same stoic will to persist recurs elsewhere, as in "Text Message," where the poet vows to "keep / death at bay," presumably with the same "modest and complicated art" that his quiet, noisy songs always involve. The great bugle-calls of the preening poets, then, have little place here; instead, the poet offers his humble "Oompahs."

Love, however, does constitute a relative exception to Droguet's skepticism with regard to exalted poetical flights of feeling, perhaps because it precludes the kind of smug solemnity that other kinds of lyrical grandiosity often involve. Human sexuality, which Droguet never censors out when he broaches the topic of romantic love—such as in "I-I-I" or "Fable of Contents"—has a built-in component of vulnerability and even awkwardness that requires a certain setting aside of the ego. Indeed, "I-I-I" stages a giving over of authority to the woman as source and foundation of the ego: "*You your word /[...] is at the root of me in truth / which is to say of my selfhood.*" Droguet's love poems, though infrequent, always bear this mark of frank humility.

Modesty, humility: human beings seem cosmically insignificant, Droguet sometimes suggests; he just as often suggests that in our tiny difference is all that is precious—God[4] is in the details:

> none here is unaware
> of the importance of *little things*
> the vaguely luminous frailty
> the fossil eternity of stars
> and what remains to laugh and sing
> is darkness utterly raw
>   ("Moderate Gale Warning")

The "luminous frailty" one might first mistake for our own, for that of some tiny human soul, finds its answer in the "fossil eternity of stars," whose fitful pinpoints seem suddenly as fragile as our own brief lives. This paradoxical identification of the vast with the tiny, the enduring with the ephemeral, the human with the cosmic, underscores the paradox of sentiment with which the poem concludes: laughter and singing are to be made only from "darkness utterly raw." Lucidity with regard to the human condition demands no less, Droguet suggests, than to forge joy and wonder directly from the stuff of our suffering and inevitable oblivion. The poet, for all his irony and skepticism, thus sets himself an ambitious task indeed.

---

4 God is a discreet but insistent presence in Droguet's poetry, often questioned; the poet remarks again on the back cover of *Maintenant ou jamais*: "There is in a few corners [...] the formidable discreet smile, the limpid and heartrending disorder of God" (my translation).

There is no darkness, in Droguet's poetry, without laughter, or wonder, or pleasure: emotions, in Droguet's work, take on complicated, changeable shapes; one hardly *feels* if not in multiple ways at once, at times in internal contradiction. I keep returning, by design, to the notion of the mixture—of emotions, but also of vocabulary and register, of languages (Droguet reads English a good deal; traces of Dante's Italian or Milton's English sometimes appear), of sublimity and irony, of clouds and waves. For Droguet returns to these mixtures also—the "broth," the "chaos," the "unkempt opera" ("Against a Dark Field")—however he names it from poem to poem. In Droguet's work, everything is a terrible, beautiful mess. And in the mix things bubble to the surface — fear and hope, suffering and sorrow, surprise and agony, disgust and rage, frustration and desire and delight.

But here I find myself caught again in the ironist's net; as soon as I lean to this side, I must lean to the other or fall into untruth. For if mess there be, the poet hardly leaves everything to chance. There is an art to the storm that we are given to thrive in. These poems grow out of notes on the hours of the sky, from jottings and observations as the day changes, but these are arranged, structured, optimized into these skeptical chamber pieces that offer us glimpses into our own bewilderment, into what Droguet calls "vertigo" in the poem "Downtime." "Vertigo" is another name for the same enchanting mess, but in that enchantment is its promise:

> the night rethickens
> each promise here is vertigo
> (or the reverse)

CLATTERS

Literally

Of what did you dream unfortunate souls
as the paving stone resounds
in time with that human stump
pummeled lacking forward marching

"of wind thrown against the willows
osiers   pine groves
that plunges and billows
a blandly greenish mist
and the wholesome scented coolness
of humid confines tender and still-
blue woods yellow heath
and the soot-black sooty crows
right true angels fair
of this unsung glen
where grasses grow green
where the brook mingles at its banks
crazed uncertain coruscations
commonplacently instantaneous"

he who has to say
his piece
his heart
muscular exuberance
and quivering fibrils
    beats and
      beats him...

December 8th, 2008

Littéralement

à quoi donc songiez-vous âmes infortunées?
quand le pavé sonne
au pas de l'humain trognon
cabossé lacunaire en marche
il va de l'avant

«au vent jeté dans les saules
osiers sapinières
qui plonge roule un brouillard
vert fadement
et la fraîcheur parfumée salubre
des humides confins tendres bois
encore bleus landes jaunes
et les bien noirs et noirs corbeaux
bons vrais bons anges
à l'ignoré vallon
où les herbes verdoient
où le ruisseau mêle en ses bords
ses irisations follement vacillantes
instantanées poncivement »

celui qui a
son mot à dire
son coeur exubérance musculaire
et frétillement des fibres
      lui bat...
      lui bat...

8 décembre 2008

Romance (suite)

1
The spectacular intermittence the illusive
immobility of a lone vagrant
alternate uncertain
ubiquitous trifle
which unscrambles itself beautifully
in the relentless
and blue sky fastidiously

the first fresh pinky rind of sunset
in frosts
the smeared profuse virulent russet
in the windfall among the bracken
soon enough the black stars
of unspent nights

and what
what backhoe scrapes scrapes
and scrapes hiccups? *okay*?

(all earthly matters unforthwith)

Roman (suite)

1
L'intermittence spectaculaire l'illusoire
immobilité d'un nuage isolé
vagabond alternatif incertain
broutille ubiquiste
qui bellement se dépatouille
dans le ciel implacable
et bleu fastidieusement

l'entame fraîche et rosie du couchant
dans les givres
l'estompé roux profus virulent
dans les chablis de la fougère aigle
bientôt les astres noirs
des nuits inépuisées

et quoi?
quoi qui sarcle sarcle
et sarcle hoquette? *okay?*

(toutes affaires incessamment terrestres)

2
keeping to yourself you would
dream and dream the frantic cartage   the flood
jumbled by oblique crosscurrents
of a river now dry
and *this dreary steppe* the guide said
once perhaps were Troy

but never mind soon
enamouring sweeps you off and takes you away
from home
and all has come to a head

January 2nd, 2009

2
et sur ton quant-à-toi tu
rêverais rêverais
l'effréné charroi le flot
brouillé d'obliques courants traversiers
d'un fleuve désormais tari
et *cette morne steppe* a dit le guide
fut peut-être un jour Troie

mais qu'importe bientôt
l'enamourement t'emporte et t'ôte
au logis
et tout est consumé

2 janvier 2009

Yarnspun

and then the werewolves all turned up
upon us they would gladly sup

they roughnecked the ghastly beasts
vacated the premises   wouldn't hold
their tongues   threw to the stiffs
clouds   arrows and rocks   snapped off
blades   nuts and bolts   foul seed
turds   snot and trash

smokily withdrawing
to glades to fallows
leered   ravaged
rimy slipped at stumps   the impure
and so it blows hardy arduous
loads upwind
to mucks muds and mires

an all migrous encrudged
passing far off
the downpour drenched their mugs
their meat their ulcers
ah! spew! christening!

and it came to an end   it was
the digging   it was
unknowing tenderness

January 22nd, 2009

À DORMIR DEBOUT

les loups-garous s'en sont venus
ils voulaient nous manger tout cru

ils s'arsouillaient les males bêtes
vidaient les lieux   ne tenaient pas
leurs langues   jetaient aux engoncés
nuages flèches et galets couteaux
démanchés cloutailles ordes semences
étrons morves et raclures

fumeusement se retranchaient
aux essarts aux jachères
guignaient   ravageaient
frimeux ripaient aux souches   les impurs
et ça tire hardi ardu
des coups des bords
aux gadoues fanges et bouillasses

toute migreuse encrugée
passante à la foraine
l'averse a lessivé leurs trognes
leurs viandes leurs ulcères
ah! dégueulis! baptême!

et cela prenait fin   c'était
le creusement   c'était
à l'insu les tendresses

22 janvier 2009

Uncertain Invention of Chasms

The scrappy wind snipes
night degerms
gravid convulsive clouds
full steam have doused the pit
and the fat sky swelters purple

will the sea have budged?
is there possibly somebody
here? is there
anyone alive?

      there's
rambling by the sputtering
flatulent urban traffic fracas
marvel of marvels anonymous
gnarl-fisted little asphalt-shaver
expecting fulminating driveller
he wanders fecundates and warbles
through vain branchy groves
powdered floured with freezes and frosts
would unbone himself   he dribbles his vainglories
tomfooleries   sticks out his tongue   reckons that
if I was just a dog
a marrow precious a happy shade...
but I'm down below meagerly
at reapings and grape-harvests
elusive exorbitant an itching god
playing hooky devours
and satiates me

February 19th, 2009

Incertaine invention des gouffres

Le vent désordonné canarde
la nuit dégerme
à toute vapeur convulsifs engrossés
les nuages ont rincé l'abîme
et le gros ciel sue pourpre

la mer aura-t-elle bougé?
y-a-t-il ici possiblement
quelqu'un? y-a-t-il
        un vivant?

       y'a
qui vadrouille au pétaradant
flatulent fracas du traffic urbain
merveille des merveilles anonyme
l'enfant rase-bitume aux poings noueux
expectant fulminant radoteur
il déambule féconde et vocalise
aux vains bosquets rameux
poudrés farinés à givres et frimas
voudrait se désosser   il bave ses glorioles
fariboles   tire sa langue   suppute que
si j'étais rien qu'un chien
précieuse moelle ombre heureuse...
mais je suis en bas menuement
aux moissons et vendanges
insaisissable exorbitant un dieu
démangé buissonnier me dévore
et me rassasie

19 février 2009

Against a Dark Field

Tanned hewn smoked have you
gnawed the bramble or the ash?
have you no
memory again of the rending happy
jaws of dream
of the hazy cleaving babble
all too charming nights!
legendary reminiscent lofts!
in the turbulent overgrown park
unkempt opera   big-boned apple-trees
where sagged theatrically
balconies balusters repositories
were heard   *furtive mellifluous
alliterations*   the howling owls the bundle
of turturtledoves' burning coo-calls

customarily each thing
stood in its place

February 22nd, 2009

A CONTRE-NUIT

Tanné fauché fumé as-tu
rongé la ronce ou la cendre?
as-tu reperdu
mémoire de l'arrachante heureuse
machoire à songe
de l'incertain bouturant babil?

trop aimables nuits!
légendaires greniers réminiscents!
au parc ensauvagé turbulent
opéra broussailleux   grands pommiers d'os
où tombaient théâtralement
balcons balustres reposoirs
s'entendaient   *allitérations furtives
melliflues*   les hiboux bouboulants l'abondant
roucoucoul enflammé des tourtours

usuellement toute chose
se tenait en sa place

22 février 2009

Passage into darkness

From the clatter
of sleep fleeing
mirrored eroded woods   chill paths
by boreal gales
some invisible animal was rutting
in an enclave
high up the spotted mistle thrush
tirelessly weaves its leitmotive
a dog digs out a mare's lung

leaden memory
undecays in tongues

February 22nd, 2009

Passage à l'obscur

Hors les boucans
du sommeil on courait
les bois mirés mordus des chemins transis
d'averses boréales
quelque animal invisible jouissait
dans une enclave
là-haut la grive philomèle ponctuée
enchaîne inlassablement ses motifs
un chien déchire un poumon de jument

la mémoire plombée
dépourrit dans les langues

22 février 2009

Congé

Many shall dreadfully be
swept away in the dark wilderness
into draining silence
into the ice floes' vague hell

yet already the impetuous mortal
fusses in the winter-room
dusty mirrors faithless shadows
before daylight he drifts away shouting
White waters! white waters! clogs and clodhoppers!

Over the fringe are harvests and raffles
snares forever for the fool who garbles and strips
inoffensive mute in a cheerless land

March 1st, 2009

Congé

Beaucoup seront terriblement
jetés hors dans les nuits sauvages
à l'épuisant silence
au vague enfer des banquises

mais déjà l'impétueux mortel
s'affaire à la chambre d'hiver
miroirs poudreux ombres feintes
avant le jour il crie s'éloignant:
Vives eaux! vives eaux! sabots et galoches!

Hors l'orée c'est cueillaisons loteries
pièges toujours au fou qui déparle et se met à nu
inoffensif aphone dans un terrain morne

1 mars 2009

Moderate Gale Warning

His back is to the wall
the traveller walks the wrong
way and his eyes riveted-steady
as it comes
on receding recent plowing
steel porticos   trailblazed fir-groves
smoky and cramped flint and millstone lodges
stretches of clay   silos silos silos
sludgy bed of a tortuous river
meagre raygrass   sometimes a tree
dry and baleful   plucked poles   stripped
masts   ferruginous copses copses
of indecipherable autumns

nothing new on the whole and all
forever and ever
beneath happy disorder
hercynian shade
bludgeons of soot in the bare ruined sky

*

Avis de grand frais

Il a le dos au mur
le voyageur il marche à contre-
sens et son oeil rivé-fixé
comme ça vient
aux fuyants frais labours
portiques d'acier   sapinaies à layons
pavillons silex et meulière étriqués et fumeux
empans de glaises   silos silos silos
lit bourbeux d'un fleuve à tortillons
raygrass maigres   un arbre quelquefois
sec et patibulaire   hampes plumées   mâts
dégarnis   boqueteaux boqueteaux ferrugineux
dans les méconnaissables automnes

rien de neuf somme toute et tout
dans les siècles des siècles
sous l'heureux désordre
l'ombre hercynienne
les massues de suie du ciel nu rompu

*

the man-whelp whose own stiff
member enkindling desire
his unpredicted predicament
enchants himself in amorous vertigo
and to celebrate empties
a flask of harsh purple wine

later he dreams on the shore
he will
        fall overhead
his heels and turns
his face upwind and spits
he wonders—yet knowing nothing
is new—at a yellow dog
shaggy waggish who yaps at the flood
tries biting the wave
and the wind turns it back
implacable
the sea kicks and coughs

none here is unaware
of the importance of *little things*
the vaguely luminous frailty
the fossil eternity of stars
and what remains to laugh and sing
is darkness utterly raw

March 5th, 2009

le petit d'homme que son membre
rigide et l'embrasant désir
inopinément turlupinent
s'enchante à l'amoureux vertige
et pour le fêter vide
un flacon d'âpre vin violet

plus tard il rêve au rivage
il va
      tomber très haut
en arrêt tourne
sa face aux souffles et crache
il s'étonne—rien pourtant
n'est jeune il le sait—d'un chien jaune
hirsute jouasse qui jappe au flot
tente mordre la vague
et le vent le rebrousse
l'implacable
la mer tousse

nul ici n'ignore
l'importance des *petits riens*
la fragilité vaguement lumineuse
l'éternité fossile des étoiles
et ce qui reste à rire et à chanter
c'est la ténèbre toute crue

5 mars 2009

Other Gardens

Buffoon executioner puppet
the paraglider at the parapet
sings hyssop and ysopet
ryegrass and autumn barley
goes quiet scampers off in a dive
gloriously *drum rum rum* glides
upon a pond   wheat-sown fields
pale vineyards   an ochre beech-grove
or some elm-islet
rusty reddened survivors
the battered wind devours and fidgets

a thicket brier-walled
munches a ruinous lodge
with squared-away cinderblocks
rafters trusses purlins
joists struts ridges and roofing
all crumbles and tumbles to dust

the mist that lulls
sinuously slumps
upon alkaline banks
of the brook cool and murky
and the silvered sidereal
minnow-fry froth and teem

March 8th, 2009

Autres jardins

Pitre bourreau marionnette
le parapentiste au parapet
chante l'hysope et l'ysopet
le fromental et l'escourgeon
se tait s'escampe à son plongeon
glorieusement *ran tan plan* plane
sur un étang   des emblavures
des vignes pâles   une ocre hêtraie
ou quelque ilot d'ormes
rouillés rougis survivants
le vent battu dévore et remuaille

un taillis mur à brousses
bouffe un pavillon ruineux
d'équarris moellons
arbalétriers fermes pannes
entraits jambes faîtages et chevrons
tout croule et roule à la poussière

la brume assoupissante
sinueusement s'écroule
aux berges alcalines
du ruisseau glauque et frais
et l'argenté sidéral
frai des vairons mousse et grouille

8 mars 2009

Clatters

For ever the spaces
expansive and infinite roar
and humpbacked or not the whales
purr their fundamental hydraulic
mishmashes and musettes
harmonically outdate the ancient thunderbolts

in the enclosed sanctuary nearby
the dedicated virgins
Godot's gang
transported heed-
lessly chant and disenchant canticles
upon canticles their pending
prayers

all the downpours have fallen
now evening the moon briskly
rises over the laurel
the wind is heard quietly
rustling in a tree
likewise without memory

March 13th, 2009

Boucans

Eternellement les espaces
expansifs infinis vrombissent
et bossues pas bossues les baleines
ronronnent leurs musettes et mixtures
hydrauliques fondamentales
harmoniquement périment les vieilles foudres

au clos sanctuaire à côté
les vierges vouées
la bande à Godot
transportées à corps
perdu chantent déchantent cantiques
sur cantiques leurs oraisons
d'attente

toutes les giboulées sont chues
désormais le soir rondement
la lune monte au-dessus du laurier
on entend le vent vaguement
dans l'arbre bruissant
comme lui sans mémoire

13 mars 2009

Bonus Poems
published with Clatters

Offshore (note)

Wondering nebulous ebullient cloudmass
the fraying effervescence of their hollows and lumps
where acid light is seeping
darkly it piles up to the north
parapet dense and numb
square soot-block suddenly falling heavy
onto the bag-lady's nurturing hide
as she wryly crosses
and uncrosses her swells

and a sea wind begins to stir
and torments us

August 9th, 2009

Au large (note)

Les émerveillants volumineux bouillons nuagiers
l'effervescence effilochée de leurs creux et bosses
où la lumière acide infuse
noirement ça s'entasse aux nords
parapet compact engourdi
carré bloc de suie soudain qui s'abat massif
à la vieille peau nourrice
qui goguenarde croise
et décroise ses houles

et le vent de la mer se lève
et nous tourmente

9 août 2009

Soliloquy

Blurred backstage   ravenous gleams
of dawns   either the buxom
unfathomable sea of words
in abeyance
and fickle flows   shambles
failing memory   dusty
attic caving in
or else *you say*   the cruel earth opened at last
too soon
dead end pit   first and final bosom
of the neither babble nor breath   full   void
or neither nor

disjointed tidings the song
flows unchecked and bubbles over
spasm   hemorrhage
epiphanic and black   *it'd better*
mention
why

January 6th, 2008

Soliloque

Confuses coulisses   dévorantes lueurs
des aurores   ou la mer
gironde insondable des mots
en souffrance
et les déferlements hasardeux   les chantiers
la mémoire invalide   le poudreux
grenier qui s'effondre
ou bien   *dis-tu*   la terre cruelle ouverte enfin
trop tôt
aveugle trou   giron premier dernier
du ni voix ni vent   plein   vide
ou ni ni

désarticulé racontar le chant
coule et dégorge à l'abandon
spasme   hémorragie
épiphanique et noire   *et faut*
que ça dise
pourquoi

6 janvier 2008

I, I, I

The woman of my life the one
to whom I wrote: *You your word*
(in every sense) revealed
from the beginning of our days-together
till the end which means
revealed to me in our time
is at the root of me in truth
which is to say of my selfhood
not in my temporary elusive essence
You and no-one else   but this
that God is asleep
on my right side and her noises various
and physiological delight me
and I place my (left) hand upon her
randomly and I land
somewhere and that's how
I sleep...or not

May 22nd, 2009

JE JE JE

La femme de ma vie   celle
à qui j'écrivais: *"Toi   ta parole*
(dans tous les sens) révélée
du commencement de nos jours-ensemble
jusqu'à la fin   c'est-à-dire
révélée à moi dans notre temps
est ce qui me fonde en vérité
c'est-à-dire encore en mon Être-Je
pas dans ma transitoire insaisissable essence
Toi et personne d'autre   mais cela
grâce à Dieu » dort
sur ma droite et ses bruits divers
et physiologiques m'enchantent
et je porte la main (gauche) sur elle
au hasard et je tombe
n'importe où   c'est ainsi
que je dors... ou pas

22 mai 2009

Shoot again (Final Ball)

God is/is not
> the woman of my life or better yet
  a real young maiden
> weekly
> sweet and sour
> hoary
> metaphysically incorrect
> craggy (just like me)
> infirm
> neither here nor there
> my brother's keeper
  (and mine)
> one-legged

HE is/is not THEREFORE I exist

(cross out whichever does not apply
cross everything out
cross nothing out
     as you wish)

April 6th, 2009

Re-jeu (pour en finir)

Dieu est / n'est pas :
> \> la femme de ma vie ou mieux encore une vraie jeune fille
> \> hebdomadaire
> \> sucré-salé
> \> chenu
> \> métaphysiquement incorrect
> \> équilatéral
> \> rocheux (tout comme moi)
> \> impotent
> \> ni fait ni à faire
> \> le gardien de mon frère
>   (et le mien)
> \> unijambiste

IL est / n'est pas DONC j'existe

(rayez les mentions inutiles
 rayez tout
 ne rayez rien
             à votre guise)

6 avril 2009

Palimpsests & Rigaudons

Tohu-bohu

in some blue too
thin some blue which nothing
is but a dream all things considered
it will have gone by too fast
the companion very fit
who sings to the fountain to the forests
the shadow the feast and the appoggiaturas

breath limit-tracing and trans-
figurative in jumps and hops
unbuilds unmasts
the frothing furious flakes
of pasteboard   soaks up and
teems in these crowds
that will fall vaguely
straight down to the liquid mirror
to the orchestral chimerical thrumming
of the inveterate swell

it will have been the last
day   it will be black like never
before

April 15, 2010

Tohu-bohu

dans du bleu peu
massif du bleu qui rien
n'est qu'un rêve au bout du compte
il sera passé trop vite
le compagnon très en jambes
qui chante à la fontaine aux fûtaies
l'ombre la bombance et les appoggiatures

le souffle délimitateur et trans-
figuratif à sauts et gambades
débâtit démâte
les écumants furieux flocons
de carton-pâte s'imbibe et
foisonne en ces cohues
qui tomberont tout
vaguement droit au liquide miroir
à l'orchestral chimérique bourdon
des flots invétérés

ç'aura été le dernier
jour ce sera le noir comme
jamais

15 avril 2010

Chimera

The simplest plain it rains there
from the sky evasive and shorn
contrapuntal
dogs yell
Monsieur de Crow caws
crows and flays

we sing the red brambles
a cloud galops and horses
of childhood (duns bays blacks
palominos chestnuts isabellines
pintos norman cobs
morgans quarter-horses)

we debone
the strange omnivorous and minute God
we roll in the Hercynian stuff
in the stuffed lexicon
we dream nothing
vague vertigos
verdant vineyard disheveled and vulpine

May 9, 2010

Chimère

La plaine simplissime il y pleut
du ciel évasif et tondu
contrapuntique
des chiens crient
Monsieur du Corbeau crabouille
craille et dépiaute

on chante les ronces rouges
un cavalant nuage et des chevaux
d'enfance (louvets bais moreaux
palominos alezans isabelle
pintos normands
morgans quarter-horses)

on désosse
l'étrange omnivore et menu Dieu
on se roule à l'hercynien fourbi
au fourbu lexique
on rêve rien
vagues vertiges
verger vert en vrac et vulpin

9 mai 2010

Fixed Point 2

Froth at his ass froth at his fangs
enraged   a dog yells at the sky
too blue to be true
which does its little dance its carnival
heroic hydrophilic of pioneer clouds
move along move along nothing to
see again here!

where is it galoping? it's rushing
rampaging in far off lands
                in next to nothing
wasting away the lovely vertigos
                it's going but to the devil
and the echo speaks
of existing *passim* if that
yet long after the end

June 20, 2010

Point fixe 2

L'écume au cul l'écume aux crocs
à la rage   un chien gueule au ciel
trop bleu pour être vrai
qui fait son cinéma sa kermesse
héroïque hydrophile de nuages pionniers
circulez circulez y'a rien
à revoir!

ça cavale où? ça se rue
se déchaîne aux là-bas
                au si peu
ça décharne les beaux vertiges
                ça va qu'au diable
et l'écho ça parle
d'exister *passim* et encore
longtemps après la fin

20 juin 2010

The Announcement

Soon enough it's the feast of Saint John
and the fire will be set
on the strand among the steppe's rockery
where the crow bustles caws and
claws down to
the wool fuzzed soiled
with grassy turds   the green and black
entrails where it buzzes and the clods
of liquid fat   the blue bones
the carcass of a *black faced* ewe
a vague pile amidst the uncertain mat
of the gramineae

and alone in the infinite
of the wide ocean   *slicing through
the frothy swell*   placed
upon the ruminating chewing sea
cormorant of periscopic neck
beneath the clouds ass to ass
burgeoning

June 29, 2010

L'ANNONCEMENT

Dans peu c'est la Saint-Jean
et l'on foutra le feu
à la grève à la steppe à rocaille
où la corneille s'affaire craille et
fouaille à même
les laines frisottées souillées
d'herbeux crottins   l'entraille verte
et noire où ça bombine et les mottes
de gras fluide   les os bleus
la carcasse d'une brebis *black face*
vague entas au hasardeux tapis
des graminées

et seul dans l'infini
du grand large   *à fendre*
les flots écumeux   posé
sur l'océan ruminant mâchouillant
un cormoran au col périscopique
sous les nuages cul à cul
qui bourgeonnent

29 juin 2010

Vademecum

necessarily subsidiary
legitimate dementia
tongue too rare and stiff
at the scull and which
sings us the true lives
ways to blather
and yada yada junk jabber

and then the night crushed
the steel twisted numerous convulsed
the galoping rumpus of the sea
rushing down and striving
and the day to come at last
to loosen its grip and calm its transports

August 16, 2010

Vademecum

nécessairement subsidiaire
légitime démence
langue trop rare et raide
à la godille et qui
nous chante les vies vraies
façons de jactance
et tagada pacotilles blablas

et puis la nuit broyée
l'acier froissé nombreux convulsé
le cavalcadant chambard de la mer
qui dévale et se décarcasse
et le jour à venir enfin
apaiser sa poigne et ses transports

16 août 2010

Once and for All

I says the other the soak
the bad thief friday
my hoohoo my who
ever and who rushes
goes without saying and takes one step
more   the last
whither and witherward ho

to the sky already almost not blue
chewed brutish the wind
the real one ends the march
wipes up dawns again and uncreases
the écru sulfate of the clouds
he feeds his anger
and the storm acid-green and tin-plated copper

the winter welters eternal
instantly
the ash is an abyss
at the end of the earth and nothingness
      undone

October 30, 2010

UNE FOIS POUR TOUTES

JE dit l'autre le boit-sans-soif
le mauvais larron vendredi
mon quiqui mon qui
conque et qui rue
va sans dire et fait un pas
de plus   le dernier
cap au père et au pire

au ciel déjà presque pas bleu
mâchonné bourru le vent
le vrai ferme la marche
ressuie les aubes et déplisse
le sulfate écru des nuages
il nourrit ses colères
et l'orage vert acide et cuivre étamé

l'hiver déferle éternel
instantanément
la cendre est un gouffre
de bout du monde et le rien
      défait

30 octobre 2010

Imprecation

Distances wretched distances
splendors mute enraged mirages
the white lightning   oh the pale
milkiness of frostbite   the energy
fierce and shredded raptor
and the impari
syllabic disorder of the vortices
the shimmering tanned wasted palimpsest
and the wordless eternity
which whitens dispossesses and deflagrates
in the sky in the cul-
de-sac in the gut cloaca
well out of
                breath

the hoarse fussing of crows
demented mantled
in the cankered windfall
somewhere a shaggy dog
shivers and coughs black
a penpusher yields to the immoderate
desire to be present   he traces
few signs   flakes
wretched illegible mira
culously
it's equally spitting in the ocean
or pissing wild in the snow

December 2, 2010

Imprécation

Lointains misérables lointains
splendeurs muettes enragés mirages
la foudre blanche   oh la pâle
laitance des gelures l'énergie
féroce et déchirée rapace
et le désordre impari
syllabique des tourbillons
le miroitant mégi dévasté palimpseste
et l'éternité sans mots
qui blanchoie dépossède et déflagre
au ciel au cul-
de-sac au boyau cloaque
à bout de
                souffle

le ramdam éraillé des corneilles
démentes mantelées
au malandreux chablis
quelque part un chien hirsute
grelotte et tousse noir
un gratte-papier cède au démesuré
désir d'être là   il trace
quelques signes   flocons
misérables illisibles mira
culeusement
c'est tout autant peigner la girafe
ou pisser sauvage à la neige

2 décembre 2010

Pot-pourri

All of it was at the beginning of things
bit of rock   a bird's footstep
the petrifying shelter of a factual cloud
the sea in the west nothing but sheet metal
in aluminium barbed tampered with
which dropped cooled threw itself at winter

two standing there
in the shortened days
the bad weather
           weathering

the pursuers the lumpy ones
with eyes bleeding with phosphenes
puffy moth-eaten
washed themselves Lord lost their way

the apostles foiled forked
excavators the promised rubbish
the killjoys they haul off
they rattle on interminably
reintone their maggot soup
their canticles their gurglings
of rancid bone and meat chunks
their tufts their carcasses
laughable and the rope to hang you with
their refrains harebrained hill of beans
and their dead words
so as to say nothing above all
it's noise

Pot-pourri

Tout c'était au début des choses
peu de pierraille   un pas d'oiseau
l'abri pétrifiant d'un nuage événementiel
la mer dans l'ouest rien qu'une tôle
d'alu trituré barbelé
qui baissait fraîchissait se jetait à l'hiver

deux qui se tenaient là
dans les jours écourtés
le gros temps
           le temps

les poursuivants les grumeleux
aux yeux sanglants à phosphènes
bouffis bouffés aux mites
se sont lavés Seigneur se sont perdus

les apôtres entravés fourchus
excavateurs les rogatons promis
les rabat-joie ils déhalent
ils dégoisent les intarissables
rentonnent leur soupe à l'asticot
leurs cantiques leurs glouglous
d'os rances et bidoches
leurs touffes leurs carcasses
à rire et la corde à s'y pendre
leurs refrains fifrelins rime à rien
et leurs mots morts
à surtout ne rien dire
c'est du bruit

                  it's best
to stay silent and seek
what is lacking in night

a year was past
the snow sprinkles flour bundles up swaddles
mille-feuilles   palimpsests crystalized
tons of silence on top
the teeming greasy cords of kelp
and black seaweed

two remain wherever
in the off-topic splendors
and the thunderous sacred fire sets them suddenly alight
leaves them helpless disordered   throws them
        one upon the other
they grab each other   climax clamoring
a hue and cry swoon   restart
            again

December 27, 2010

        le mieux
c'est se taire et chercher
ce qui manque à la nuit

une année fut passée
la neige ça farine engonce emmitouffle
mille-feuilles   palimpsestes cristallisés
des tonnes de silence par-dessus
le cordon grouillant gras des laminaires
et des noirs goémons

deux restent n'importe où
dans les splendeurs hors-sujet
et le feu sacré foudreux soudain les embrase
les désempare les désordonne   l'un à
      l'autre les jette
ils s'empoignent   jouissent à cru
et à cris se pâment   remettent
          ça

27 décembre 2010

Declensions

Displaced replaced placed in the world   over
thrown   —*let the feasting and recounting
down commence!*—
soon screwed
              outside
the vague eye unblurred
cheeks of cardboard glabrous and grey
least and seedy
crowd over there toward a blue ark
and the isle of pink burnet
they've shared winters
and field for field their abyss
delicious exile   they've pissed
into the wind   crushed *frrt frrt* the snows
given signs
              irresistably

trace for forgetting   rarefied lure for nothing
feinted farce bilking grief
it disfigures   it meddles
it doesn't cost a thing

May 29, 2011

Déclinaisons

Démis remis mis au monde   jetés
bas —*que la fête et le conte*
à rebours commencent!—
bientôt foutus
             dehors
l'oeil vague débrouillé
joues de carton glabre et gris
moindres et miteux
cohue là-bas vers une arche bleue
et l'île aux roses pimprenelles
ils ont partagé les hivers
et champ contre champ leur abîme
l'exil délicieux   ont fait leur pipi
contre le vent   pilé *frrt frrt* les neiges
fait signe
             irrésistiblement

trace à l'oubli   raréfié leurre à rien
feinte farce et trompe deuil
ça défigure   ça s'immisce
ça mange pas de pain

29 mai 2011

Frolic

sibilant the wind
has split hares
wiped off the wild opacity again
from the forest restored dismantled

fistfuls of ashes
sour impalpable powder to chew up again
in the cardamine and the dandelion
percolating swish
disheveled wall of the plumed waters
hairy masks and mugs
slimy dripping

so little to little to none
the scent of camphor and ether
in God's cabin
at the hour when through the snow amiably
the wolves go off to confession

eye in a dive uncertain hand
dead tongue   freaky clerk dread-
stammering scribe paper scraper
wandering mail officer pen
pusher gone rancid boiled from head to toe
scarecrow and bundle punter
of falsehoods and dreamery
go on! print-seller! bugger against
the earth   go on! beggar's bag
we can hear them again your lapping your fabrication
and that's all   you can
gulp your hooch and sing the cruise
it all goes wrong! it all goes wrong!
The scribble's on the wall

August 13, 2011

Folâtrerie

sibilant le vent
a coupé les chevaux en quatre
ressuyé l'opacité sauvage
de la forêt ravalée débâtie

cendres empoignées
aigre impalpable poudre à remâcher
dans la cardamine et la dent-de-lion
chuintis percolateur
mur ébouriffé des eaux panachées
masques poilus et trognes
limonées goutelantes

si peu que peu que rien
le parfum de camphre et d'éther
dans la baraque à Dieu
à l'heure où par la neige aimablement
les loups s'en vont-à-confesse

oeil à la plonge main confuse
langue morte   insolite greffier redou-
balbutable scribe gratte papier
vagant vaguemestre rond-
de-cuir ranci bouilli de pied en cap
épouvantail et fagot brelandier
de menteries rêvassures
va donc! imagier! bougre à ras
de terre   va donc! besace
on les rentend tes laperies tes fabriques
et c'est tout   tu peux
siffler ta goutte et chanter la croisière
rien ne va plus! rien ne va plus!
Les jeux sont tout défaits

13 août 2011

Rusticities

at night   no more nature
the great births the neolithic
angels pass through the fury
and the confused intoxication of the gusts
and keep silent finally
the way a child dies
their fierce and magnificent weakness
pleases the old dead men rogues and kings
prophets poets with brouettes
and the bellowing ones
the powers that be
whose giblets whose bones whiten
and fall into sepulchers of nothing

enormous potbellied lively
broth the ocean moves
flows with folly and fracas
beneath the ruffled sulfur sky
rocks and blocks all this stuccos and sheetrock
smeared spread with wipings the color of rhubarb

it is the tranquil hour when copiously
a cow pisses in the fog

January 26, 2012

Rusticités

la nuit   plus de nature
les grandes naissances   les anges
néolithiques passent dans les fureurs
et la confuse ivresse des bourrasques
et se taisent enfin
comme un enfant meurt
leur faiblesse magnifique et farouche
a réjoui les vieux morts gueux et rois
prophètes poètes à brouettes
et les brailleurs
les puissants de la terre
de qui les abattis les os blanchissent
et tombent aux sépulcres à rien

énorme ventru vif
bouillon l'océan bouge
fracasse et flue follement
sous le ciel de traîne et de soufre
rocs et blocs tout ça stucs et staffs
confiturés tartinés d'essuillures couleur de rhubarbe

c'est l'heure tranquille où copieusement
une vache pisse dans le brouillard

26 janvier 2012

Before Going Out

at the short shadows at twilight
peak hours and off-peak
fleeting run run
irreparably and the blind clockmaker
is all ears   the happy furious
gurgling of the fountains

the day ungilds   the wind
blackens its snarl
settles its scores
and the sky blue grainy
hairy hill collapses

night carcass the sea frizzy
uncorked snotty
rushes in and stinks it's
the black clacking and cracking tongue
on the other side of the world

at the source
a snake bites its tail again

February 9, 2012

Avant la sortie

aux courtes ombres au crépuscule
les heures pleines creuses
et fugitives courent courent
irréparablement et l'aveugle horloger
écoute toute ouïe   le borborygme
heureux furibond des fontaines

le jour dédore   le vent
noircit ses hargnes
règle ses comptes
et le ciel colline bleue grenue
poilue s'effondre

carcasse à nuit la mer crépue
débondée muqueuse
s'engouffre et pue c'est
la noire langue claquetante
et craqueuse de l'autre côté du monde

à la source
un serpent se remord la queue

9 février 2012

On the Way

Tonight it's winter
and the immaculate black   gallows cross
gibbet in the tussle
and the enigmatic foofaraw of the snows
and the cloudbursts

he who was coming is on the way and shall come
to hold the door open for the flesh
purified desiring and dreaming
the fire without foreplay   destined
mechanical
and the wine is cool

astern! astern to all
as they don't say
there is a polar place
of froth to flee   to a blessed
place to stand at a halt
vaguely in love

yet all have feared these domains
a restricted wall collapses
a mediocre rain vaguely lisps scratches
the lake of signs
no one speaks any longer

EN ROUTE

Cette nuit c'est l'hiver
et le noir immaculé échafaud croix
potence dans l'empoigne
et l'énigmatique hourvari des neiges
et des trombes

qui venait est en route et viendra
tenir porte ouverte à la chair
purifiée désirante et rêveuse
la fougue sans apprêts fatale
        mécanique
et le vin est frais

arrière! arrière à tout
comme on ne dirait pas
il est polairement un lieu
d'écume où fuir un lieu
béni où se tenir dans la halte
et le vague amour

tous ont craint pourtant ces domaines
un mur restreint s'effondre
une pluie médiocre vaguement zézaie gratte
le lac des signes
on ne parle plus

seeing what day it is now in the morning
twenty-four thousand five hundred
ninety-eighth
it's moving on to storms
the paradise-breaking universe and the evil
it is said   it's brand new no more kneeling
nor marks of infamy   blow the fanfare!
Awake unheard-of brass
timpani rootatoots
Farewell! farewell for the idol
with its snout trunk beards and trappings
laughter and rage necessary and lost
trust it
weary crowds on the way
and bearing straight everywhere

and let's move on you know to the downpours

March 2, 2012

au jour qu'il est maintenant au matin
vingt-quatre mille cinq cent
quatre-vingt dix-huitième
on passe aux tempêtes
l'univers brise-grâce et le mal
on dit *c'est tout neuf   plus d'à genoux*
ni de flétrissures   allez la fanfare!
Éveillez-vous cuivres inouis
timballes ronflonflons
congé! congé pour l'idole
à groin trompe barbes et bardas
le rire et la rage nécessaires et perdus
fiez-vous z'y
lasses foules en route
et cap tout partout

et passons sais-tu aux averses

2 mars 2012

Real Label on a Simulated Bottle

downpours and lulls
the crazy proverbs
the lovely girls strolling and the happy gallants
have you seen do think on it
the phaneroptera
the ephippiger and the oedipoda?

on the fields everywhere
yet it's a boon
anemones narcissus and the grass
small cool   the gathered
flake of the carnations
the seething the sounding foliage
in the half-dusks
when the wind picks a fight
and when madly—ah! what singsong—
the linnet squeaks again

in any and all foam
unheard-of solitudes are invented
and formerly the sky the high ups
grey black cabbage green
the minced blue leaf
of the sea
        down here
        it was all one

March 13, 2012

Etiquette vraie sur une bouteille feinte

trombes et bonaces
les fous proverbes
les belles flâneuses et les heureux galants
as-tu vu songes-z'y
bien le phanéroptère
l'éphippigère et l'oedipode?

sur les prés partout
c'est pourtant l'aubaine
anémones narcisses et l'herbe
menue fraîche   le flocon
froncé des oeillets
les houleux les sonnants feuillages
dans les demi-soirs
quand le vent mène son estrif
et qu'éperduement—ah! les chanteries—
rapiâle la linotte

par toutes les écumes
s'inventent d'inouïes solitudes
et le ci-devant ciel les là-hauts
gris noirs verts chou
l'émincé feuillet bleu
de la mer
        ici-bas ce fut
        tout un

13 mars 2012

A Life

at his functus misstep
gloriously little by little
body bio
degradable he goes
my furry perambulator
my bristly one my ninny
ember rupture vertigo
and small too
quite immortal soul
marionnette pirouette
he re-goes

dawn the washerwoman
blunderbuss in them azures
throws its thin minced
yellow rays
upon the woods singy dingy fringy
that shimmer to the skies
thin abyss vestiary mineral and fossil
past present future of the clouds

April 7, 2012

Une vie

à son faux pas désaisi
glorieusement petit à petit
corps bio
dégradable il va
mon velu préambulateur
mon hérissé ma nunuche
braise brisure vertige
et petite itou
très immortelle âme
marionnette pirouette cacahouète
il re va

l'aube la blanchisseuse
tromblon dans les zazurs
jette ses minces hachés
rayons jaunes
au bois roussi sombri verdi
qui poudroie aux cieux
maigre abîme vestiaire minéral et fossile
des nuages passés présents futurs

7 avril 2012

Factory

he who shall not go
further here he is who
scours the mirror's
depths he runs to the foreshor
tened distance   mismatches and dreams
his outlandish life
unrecounts his delights

the encysted stubby planetrees
with warts and varicose veins
at the edge of the deserted streets

the brawl and the truculent belligerent
reign by picks and spikes of the crows
over the seething sack of entrails
of a very very dead hare
in the muddled splendor of the sainfoin

then in the green hollow where the photons foam
the windy lowbellied kind the foal
which rushes to the rocky water's edge and their laughter
exorbitant black wild
and here dies the bitter columbine
a cloud dissipates
the horizon's running out

that's
      all

May 6, 2012

Manufacture

celui qui n'ira pas
plus loin voici qu'il
défouille un fond
de miroir il court à l'estran
gement   dépareille et rêve
sa vie à coucher dehors
déconte ses délices

les enkystés trognoneux platanes
à verrues et varices
au bord des rues désertes

la bagarre et l'hargneux gouailleur
règne à pic et pioche des corbeaux
sur le bouillonnant sac d'entrailles
d'un lièvre très très mort
dans la splendeur confuse des sainfoins

puis au val vert qui mousse de photons
genre ventu ventru le poulain
qui fringue au bord des eaux à rocaille et leur rire
exorbitant noir sauvage
et voici mourir l'amère ancolie
un nuage se dissipe
l'horizon vient à manquer

voilà
    tout

6 mai 2012

To Name Names

So at night a hutch of fogs
shadows maelstroms
and bad dreams
the violent splendor forgotten
milky of galaxies
giant red super
novas and nebulae

and beneath the sky sulphur and mercury
the powder mills wardrobes of clouds
rags and togs
the wandering fellow   de-nominated
         So and so
sees yet another day appear
the thick light strangely
frothy of dawn over the estuary
from which ascends a brig under reduced sail

the wind turns around
the lapping grows stronger
shrouds and topping lifts click and clack
a lizard seals himself in
under the polypods the blue peppermint
the cattails
slendy seedy jade-green penny-pies
the crazy frenzied
jubilant polyphony
of birds can be heard
and the modest counterpoint of the cuckoo

Noms de noms

La nuit donc un vaisselier de brouillards
d'ombres de tourbillons
et de mauvais songes
la splendeur violente oubliée
laiteuse des galaxies
géantes rouges super
novas et nébuleuses

et sous le ciel sulfure et mercure
les poudreries penderies de nuages
frusques et loques
le quidam errant   le dé-nommé
         Untel
voit paraître un jour encore
la lumière épaisse étrangement
moussue de l'aube sur l'estuaire
qu'un brick sous-toilé remonte

le vent dévire
le clapot forçit
haubans et balancines cliquent et claquent
un lézard se calfeutre
sous les polypodes les menthes
poivrées bleues les hampes à quenouilles
effilées grenaillues des ombilics vert jade
s'entend la folle
effrénée jubilante
polyphonie oiselière
et le contrepoint circonspect du coucou

the walker pisses all over a sublunary embankment
sprawls out among the grass   daydreams   scrawls:

> *I is a not-there*
>
> *it's good to die*
> *at the end of one's life*
> *rather than the beginning*
>
> *and these cartfuls of centuries*
> *it's nothing less than*
> *five minutes of wind*

May 19, 2012

le piéton compisse un talus sublunaire
s'étend parmi les herbes   songe   griffonne

    je est un hôte

    il est bon de mourir
    à la fin de sa vie
    plutôt qu'au début

    et ces charretées de siècles
    c'est rien moins que
    cinq minutes de vent

19 mai 2012

Fable of Contents

outside mother-of-pearl and phosphorous it's
the sky hot to boiling
the lightning all of a sudden black
the arduous glaucous pestle of the sea
ragged moaning the backwash
the rain the rain the rain
that rags and rogues and gloats
refrigerates the hazy outlines
fens heaths and bogs

it has soon been five hours
a window opens   another
has closed
a convoy ratatat rolls in a yard

lightly the lady
straddles the lover
they mingle and put
their hearts more and more
into it
they come
the man had said   *I don't know*
where I'm going but this
at least I know
and it's the only thing
in truth that I still know

June 4, 2012

Fable des matières

dehors nacre et phosphore c'est
le ciel chaud bouillant
la foudre tout-à-coup noire
l'ardu glauque pilon de la mer
loqueux râleux le ressac
la pluie la pluie la pluie
qui rague et rogue et glotte
réfrigère les indécis modelés
des brennes des brandes et des varennes

il a été bientôt cinq heures
une fenêtre s'ouvre   une autre
s'est fermée
un convoi tacatant roule dans un triage

légèrement la femme
enfourche l'aimé
ils s'emmêlent et mettent
du coeur encore et encore
à l'ouvrage
ils jouissent
l'homme avait dit   *j'ignore*
où je vais mais cela
du moins je le sais
et c'est la seule chose
au vrai que je sache encore

4 juin 2012

Sketches in My Red Zap Book

Quatuor no. 3

All in chaos   crumbled
cankered boiled coppery
scaly sill   tossle
of opal silks and mauve
cleft of gold goateed feathery
purlings and darnings
that's all the sky is   chaos of mud blender
polychromatic ice creamery where the grey
the slate blue horizon the honeyed
plumbing-gold steep trickle
the shadows' luminous refrigerations
and Betelgeuse blushing unto death

March 28, 2013

Quatuor n° 3

Tout en chaos   croustillé
chancreux bouillu cuivreux
seuil feuilleté   touillis
de soies opale et mauves
brèche d'or plumetée barbichue
tricotis et remaillures
c'est que ça le ciel   chaos de boue mixeur
polychrome sorbetière où le gris
le bleu ardoise horizon l'or
miellé plombagineux infusent perfusent
les congélations lumineuses des ombres
et rouge à mourir Bételgeuse

28 mars 2013

Text Message

The more than imperfect wind the vigorous breeze
Murmur fracture frizzle with loons
sweeps golden acres uncrosses
the waves hurried rhythmic
formidably then
wearily ravages and dismantles
the hirsute hercynian
grass askew the greasy spoons
baubles & barnacles and it's
the half-light vermillion bullion
the already uncertain clarity that grows dim
in the permeable thick shadow
of the undergrowth

congested barbed bearded advancing
the clouds unwind
their story ferociously free without
figures without plots nor
beginnings nor
                    endings

there is always in the dark
a distant storm preparing to
pounce disturb shear
the sea where the brill
the houndshark the conger
and the monkfish eat each other

Texto

Le vent plus qu'imparfait la brise drue
murmure brisure friture à lanturlus
balaie des arpents d'or décroise
les flots précipités rythmiques
formidablement puis
lassement ravage et démantèle
l'hirsute hercynienne
herbe de guingois les guinguettes
breloques & berniques et c'est
le demi-jour lingot vermillon
l'incertaine clarté déjà qui s'exténue
dans l'ombre perméable épaisse
d'un sous-bois

congestionnés barbelés barbus qui s'avancent
les nuages déroulent
leur histoire farouchement libre sans
figures sans intrigues ni
commencement ni
                fin

il y a toujours dans le noir
un orage lointain qui s'apprête à
bondir désordonner tondre
la mer où s'entremangent
la barbue l'émissole
le congre et la baudroie

a gibbet creaks
the crows hush distinctly
the gorse the cuckoos the daffodils
flower the edge of the narrow stream
that you step right over
an oiltanker lows in the fog
that smells like milk ensiled feed horsehair
of the animals in the field
a blue dog furtive and faerie
licks its chops

        ***

November night vigil
in the land of papuatry
        already
    someone is dying
        their good death
we stand there more and more
like a chicken on
a barrel of tar
we love—*ah! the happy sighs*
      and the soothing vertigo!—
we write at breakneck speed
to find the proper usage
for silence to un/say
and keep
    death at bay.

November 12, 2016

un gibet grince
les corneilles se taisent net
les ajoncs les coucous les jonquilles
fleurissent le bord de l'étroit ruisseau
qu'on enjambe d'un pas
un pétrolier meugle dans la brume
qui sent le lait le fourrage ensilé le crin
des chevaux au pré
un chien bleu furtif et chimère
liche ses badigoinces

***

novembre la nuit la veille
au pays de papoésie
                    déjà
  quelqu'un meurt
              de sa belle mort
on se tient là encore et encore
comme une poule sur
un tonneau de goudron
on aime—*ah! les heureux soupirs*
        et l'apaisant vertige!—
on écrit à tombeau ouvert pour
trouver le bon usage
du silence se dé/dire
et tenir
      la mort à distance.

12 novembre 2016

In the Ancient Manner

dry rain oakum
pitch asphalt & coal tar
hospice mon bel hospice
etcetera
(scrap flotsam metaphorical
rags nothing)

the common lot it
hangs from my your thy
nose   it's right before my your thine
eyes

yet it will take me you
us
        by surprise

BUT
*(antistrophe and back-
pedalling)*

barbed day has more
or less risen
all the birds from here holler
in unison break back in
with their yammer monodies
their hymns fanfares
counterpoint

and it shall never end

February 24, 2017

À L'ANCIENNE

pluie sèche étoupe
brai bitume & coaltar
mouroir mon beau mouroir
et coetera
(bataclan bazar oripeaux
métaphoriques rien)

le lot commun cela
me te vous pend
au nez   me te vous crève
les yeux

cela pourtant me te
nous prendra
    par surprise

MAIS
(*antistrophe et retro-
pédalage*)

c'est jour pointu plus
ou moins venu
tous les oiseaux d'ici s'égosillent
à l'unisson rentament
leurs caquets monodies
leurs hymnes fanfares
contrepoints

et cela n'aura pas de fin

24 février 2017

UPDATE

Spundried shaken wisps
drunk on nothing naked frantic
jostled lost to toppling
blessed fallen
from the sky everything fallen
from the phenomenal belly of the trans
ascendental bi trans
gender and all God

the small small worlds
coaldust rinsed scrubbed in the splendor
full and loose resounding
with a storm and what
do you know the categorical
sky has a grand air
where the sun is now
but a waste rough plaster

the light blurred
quits dislodges
the air lightens   a cloud
green unstable fidgets
in the meadow grass through
a blue thicket there's swishing
the cemetery is a big sad
store and the sweetness after

Mise à jour

Essorés secoués fétus
ivres à rien nus éperdus
bousculés perdus à la bascule
bénis tombés
du ciel tout tombé
du bedon phénoménal du trans
ascendental bi trans
genre et tout Dieu

les petits petits mondes
poussier rincé lessivé dans la splendeur
pleine et déliée sonnante
d'un orage et voilà-t-
il pas que le ciel
catégorique a grand air
où le soleil n'est plus
que gâchis plâtre bourru

la lumière brouillée
renonce se dépayse
l'air s'allège   un nuage
vert instable bougeotte
au pré dans l'herbe à la traverse
dans un fourré bleu ça froufroute
le cimetière est un grand magasin
triste et la douceur d'après

the swell rubs away a castle
of sand and the errant machinery
of floods trims a cliff
where set upon set free in the great outside
floats a man
hat of blue straw yellow ribbon
he's there not there   dispensing pensive
ripping out thought   reaffixing
the unknown   the dizziness   and it's all
                       one

April 15, 2017

le flot efface un château
de sable et la mécanique errante
des déluges émonde une falaise
où livré délivré dans les grands dehors
flotte un homme
chapeau de paille bleue ruban jaune
il est là pas là   à dépenser pensif
arrachant la pensée refixant
l'inconnu   les vertiges   et c'est tout
        un

15 avril 2017

Artist's Trial

The wind in the west rips up rushes in
in the beauty brief perfect and dense
of a sluggish cumulonimbus
and it's raining drearily
on some dirt acres
of felt and the snowbells
the sea holly and the dog roses
where all alone goes a snail
who isn't faint of heart
and knows neither impatience nor
love love which is
the other name for vertigo

*

forty snows pass
in the depths of the shopkeeper shadow
where people count noiselessly
some chairs
and ramble

*

The sun all at once
just once is wafer
& clot of plaster in the sky slip
shod workday tarred
dull lead and anthracite yellow
changing yarns
and the storm-sowing machine
sways and lisps   dusk
shades in blue an ocre and red field

Épreuve d'artiste

Le vent dans l'ouest dépave s'engouffre
dans la beauté brève parfaite et dense
d'un cumulo-nimbus pantouflard
et ça pleut mornement
sur de la terre des arpents
de feutre et les soldanelles
les panicauts et les cynorrhodons
où s'en va tout seul un escargot
qui n'a pas froid aux yeux
et ne connaît ni l'impatience ni
l'amour l'amour qui est
l'autre nom du vertige

*

quarante neiges passent
au fond de la ténèbre boutiquière
où des gens comptent sans un bruit
des chaises
et glosent

*

Le soleil d'un seul coup
d'un seul c'est pastille
& caillot de plâtre au ciel à tort
et à travers ouvrable goudronné
plomb mat et jaune anthracite
qui change de laines
et la machine à foudre y
zigzague et zézaie le soir
bleuit un champ ocre et rouge

the child nose in the water
measures the sea inert molasses
compote when it's clock calm
emerald untidy starch
*that looks like nothing at all**
he sees it roll its muscles
beyond the reefs   block on the verge
of exploding
when an imperceptible breeze
revives its fury however
he would like to untwist it
stuttering Tom Thumb and prey
word for word to words words
rewords rejects mellow
beloved muttered moppets

* *Georges Perros*

November 16, 2017

l'enfant museau dans l'eau
mesure la mer mélasse inerte
compotis quand ça *pétole*
empois désordonné d'émeraude
*qui ne ressemble à rien**
il la voit rouler ses muscles
au-delà des écueils   bloc au bord
d'exploser
quand un souffle insensible
anime pourtant sa fureur
il aimerait la détordre
petit poucet bègue et proie
mot à mot des mots mots
remots rebuts savoureux
chéris marmots marmonnés

* *Georges Perros*

16 novembre 2017

Brief

we're almost there
twisted-crooked-composted-deboned-detailed
mute
on the road quiet leafy
in great shadow

we fall into silence
and the sky one storm later
jumps out at you   we jump
to the clearing & very far away
toward forgetting the gust rips a fence
out of joint   the rain *nunc et semper*
rinces my snout
and *thank God* nature
is there   stinking
marvelously

November 16, 2017

Bref

on est là presque
tordu-crochu-composté-désossé-équeuté
mutique
au chemin tu feuillu
à la grande ombre

on court au silence
et le ciel un orage plus tard
saute aux yeux   on saute
à la clairière & très loin
vers l'oubli la bourrasque dégonde
une barrière   la pluie *nunc et semper*
me rince la gueule
et *Dieu merci* la nature
est là   puante
merveilleusement

16 novembre 2017

Ritornello

the gloom humid in the dusks
the unheard-of black broken silence
of the dark precursor
to ensue the fire forked thrown
the dazzling hairy chaos which
multiplinfinites everywhere a pond masked
by beeches more or less
copper rocks blue green
yellow and red a suburb
with bungalows and worlds
visible and in-

the moon is full and crimson
we must wait for the winter wind to howl
(jackdaws rooks crows)
forgotten far away
            ...and the thaw

this new old world
weary in the end
the one that sings in the delights
of love—towing full
tilt reason retinkered—
and who like every
one goes off to the white
n' black wall
for dying *takes* training
        takes
                a lifetime

December 16, 2017

Ritournelle

la ténèbre humide dans les soirs
l'inouï noir silence rompu
du précurseur sombre
à s'ensuivre le feu fourchu jeté
le fulgurant chaos chevelu qui
démultiplillimite la trace prescrite
illumine partout un étang masqué
de hêtres plus ou moins
pourpres des rocs bleus verts
jaunes et rouges une banlieue
à pavillons et les mondes
visibles & pas

la lune est pleine et rousse
il faut attendre qu'hurle le vent d'hiver
(choucas freux corneilles)
oublié lointain
        ... et le dégel

ce monde neuf ancien
lasse à la fin
celui qui chante dans les délices
de l'amour—déhalage à tout
va raison qu'on rinvente—
et qui comme tout
un chacun s'en va au mur blanc
zet noir
car mourir *s'apprend*
     ça prend
          toute une vie

16 décembre 2017

Snapshot

Night stutters   it's
bit by bit
lucerne and faggots
the cloudy dream crudely
there in the scent delight

slow voracious fine
job a downpour slantwise
strafes a reach red encrusted
slaps against a pier
the sea that gibbet
laps hammers chews

in alleys in garrets
the wind turns and what
king adrift strung up
cleft   *ad libitum*
comes goes
         goes out again?

December 22, 2017

Cliché

La nuit bégaie   c'est
à petit feu
luzerne et fagot
les nuageux rêvent cru
là-bas dans l'odeur délice

lente vorace belle
ouvrage une averse en biais
mitraille un bief croûté rouge
claque sur un ponton
la mer cette potence
lape cogne mâchonne

à ruelle à grenier
le vent tourne et quel
roi perdu pendu
fendu *ad libitum*
va vient
        s'en reva?

22 décembre 2017

Machinery 2

The days are all black
in the devil's pocket
and it's morning it's evening it's raining
shadow it's dusk you put
one foot in front of the other and the other
in front of the one until
the sea real omnipresent
bristling slate quarry   roly-poly dump &
omnibus that grumbles drubs
crumbles and daubs
there the heave has
an unfilled belly
rustling wrinkle and slurry
pallidly green which burrows snoops
hurries and hisses swells
       its gut
       and sands
rocks tirelessly

you stay there in the gaps
and the red-blond ochre thatching
of the cut off ferns
gripe:
   "Nanny nitpickers
   Husband-pickers
   Take good care
   Gleaners everywhere
   Farewell red slippers
   Farewell my lovers"

Machinerie 2

Les jours sont tout noirs
dans la poche du diable
et c'est le matin c'est le soir il pleut
de l'ombre c'est le crépuscule on met
un pied devant l'autre et l'autre
devant l'un jusqu'à
la mer réelle omniprésente
ardoisière hérissée   dodu foutoir &
fourre-tout qui grognonne cogne
fragmente et peinturlure
là-bas la houle a
le ventre creux
bruissante froissure et laitance
verte pâlement qui fouit fouine
grouille et chuinte enfle
  sa panse
  et ponce
des rocs infatigablement

on se tient là   dans les écarts
et l'ocre blond rouquin chaume
des fougères tranchées *rasibus*
à dégoiser:
 «Chercheuses de poux
 Chercheuses d'époux
 Prenez garde à vous
 Glaneuses flaneuses
 Adieu souliers rouges
 Adieu les zamours »

small change it's the grass
(poor is its muffled way
of being in the shadows
roving and the golden hereafter
morning world) the grass then
the carpet bugleweed and the horned poppy
grows green in a railyard
where the multiplied impacts
of the ratatat convoys
ram down the stopblocks

a horse dappled boiled cardboard blue
is hooked in a tree
bushy bundle of beams and twitterings
the friend sips (*Cheers and health*)
three drops of red wine
out of the rain gentle happy scale
out of hazard azure in the tilled turned sky
the luminous electron flows
a cloud exactly square
barks (I hear it) the lightning
in violet makes the chickadees tremble
it's going to rain again   trickle
quivering on the steeples
the mires and the moats
where floats a bird black
                and dead

menue monnaie c'est l'herbe
(pauvre est son mode assourdi
d'exister dans l'ombre
buissonnière et le doré navrant
monde au matin) l'herbe donc
la bugle rampante et le pavot cornu
verdoie dans un dépôt ferroviaire
où les impacts multipliés
des tacatacants convois
tamponnent des heurtoirs

un cheval pommelé bleu de carton bouilli
est croché dans un arbre
fagot touffu de rayons et cuicuis
l'ami sirotte (*Paix et santé*)
trois gouttes de vin rouge
hors la pluie gamme légère heureuse
hors l'hasard et l'azur au ciel bêché remué
les flux lumineux d'électrons
un nuage exactement carré
aboie (je l'entends) un éclair
violet fait trembler les mésanges
il va repleuvoir   ruisselis
frissoulis sur les clochers
les fanges et les douves
où flotte un oiseau noir
    et mort

the artillery the deep fry fool
raging truck the talk
outbound squall
of the destabilizing winds
rebounding sarabands vaultings
it rends gnashes blurs
pluperfectly it slips
its tongues through the cracks
of the last outskirts
of the seekings the nothings

                        it's
vitrifying dawn in the peatbog
in the treefrogs' fiddle the craaa
of the coal crow of the bleak rook
the black beast skirls in the woods
homo homo forlorn mammal
trims his hair or not depending
he laughs hollow and darkly
he kills the fatted calf
measures the wind
sings your mingled dust
the wild raz and the breeze
the bitter muck the doorjambs...
trains run through the plain
a cancerous ant dies

l'artillerie le graillon fou
rageant fourgon la parlotte
survente à la partance
des souffles déstabilisateurs
à rebonds sarabandes voltiges
ça rache grinche floute
plus-que-parfaitement ça roule
ses pelles ses galoches
aux dernières lisières
aux chercheries aux riens

                c'est
la vitrifiante aube à la tourbière
dans le crincrin des rainettes le *crâââ*
du corbac black du funèbre freux
la noire bête huche dans la fûtaie
homo homo triste mammifère
taille son poil ou pas selon
il rit jaune et noir
il tue le veau gras
mesure le vent
chante vos poudres emmêlées
le raz sauvage et le poussier
l'amère gadoue les chambranles...
des trains courent la plaine
une fourmi cancéreuse meurt

the dazed brute escapee angel
will have come to feel the wind
set sail & grasp at the water again
cold and black
all this child's play

August 11, 2017

la brute éblouie l'évadé l'ange
sera venu prendre le vent
le large & rempoigner l'eau
froide et noire
tout ça jeu d'enfant

11 août 2017

Orpheus

    came from nearby
has
    scratched at his hinges
    at nails gnawed left bleeding
    mask upon mask
    and soothed again hobbled
    on a heath

has
    not wept at the neap tide
    come in the white dawn
    and the foreign oats the grass
    of the deceased and the counterpoint
    of a bird
            over there

has
    beaten the brush and the pavement
    while it's hot
    stretched the cloud taut
    limped his love song
    warbled his hum in unison
    diddledum

has
  un
  sung down the primrose path
  in the land bitten slept
  black

Orphée

    venu de pas loin
a
    gratté ses charnières
    à sang rongé quitté
    masque sur masque
    et rapaisé boité
    sur une brande

a
    pas pleuré à la morte eau
    joui dans la blanche aube
    et l'avoine étrangère l'herbe
    des trépassés et le contre-chant
    d'un oiseau
            par là

a
    battu la campagne et le pavé
    pendant qu'il est chaud
    tiré le nuage au carré
    claudiqué sa romance
    fait son ronron unisson
    patapon

a
    dé
    chanté la prétentaine
    au pays mordu dormi
    noir

   has
     sought nothing

   has
      n't managed

   has
     gouged out his eyes   turn
     ing back
          cried out

December 22, 2017

a
   rien cherché

a
   pas pu

a
   troué ses yeux   se re
   tournant
             crié

22 décembre 2017

Figure

guano skies
strange laundry all accounts
settled that fall
to the waters white and humpbacked
enormous bowel and turmoil

words are tenacious foam
and a bit of bone left run of the mill
without memory or some horsehair
lackluster shimmer &
pittance bare   murmur
to nothing
              it's a desert
shear and ash again and
always ash

December 22, 2017

Figure

ciel à guano
linge étrange pour solde
de tout compte qui tombe
aux eaux bossues blanches
énorme entraille et grouillement

les mots c'est tenace écume
et de l'os resté tout venant
sans mémoire ou du crin
miroitement terne &
nue pitance   murmure
à rien
     c'est désert
cisaille et cendre encore et
toujours cendre

22 décembre 2017

I haven't said my final word

Prehistoric winds trounce
the leafy bouillon
feathery green and copper of the bald cypress trees
(*toxodium distichum*)
they plowshare scratch
to the bone the additional nights
omnivorous voracious the waters
rise the waters
               sink

to the fog without
contour nor color
to the gleaning to the deep it's
a cry—*dream soul nerves*—
in the shadow somewhere
near death
it's the unseen the impalpable
cloud-blue ass on the fence

the harsh sliver of silence too
but the long rain re-rain
on the regrowth and the sprouting stone   the din
of city outskirts stinking bitterly it's
the cluttered dawn muddled
in a cool corner
the spring the scent mixed
with scales courtyards sour milt
the children
        passion misfortune and delight
         sweetness and bite
                  have grown pale

February 10, 2018

Je n'ai pas dit mon dernier mot

Des vents de préhistoire étrillent
le bouillon feuillu
plumeux vert et cuivre des cyprès chauves
(*toxodium distichum*)
ils charruent grattent
à l'os les nuits supplémentaires
omnivores voraces les eaux
montent les eaux
             descendent

à la brume sans
contours ni couleurs
à la glane au profond c'est
un cri—*rêve âme nerfs*—
dans l'ombre quelque part
du côté de la mort
c'est l'inaperçu l'impalpable
bleu nuage au cul entre deux chaises

l'âpre écharde du silence aussi
mais la longue pluie repluie
sur le regain et la pierre germée   le fracas
d'un faubourg à puer âcrement c'est
l'aube encombrée confuse
dans un coin de fraîcheur
le printemps l'odeur mêlée
d'écaille de préau de laitance aigre
les enfants
    passion poisse et délices
    douceur et morsures
                ont pâli

10 février 2018

Precipitations

Rain steam and speed

Unexpected use of the sky
pure bare raw   raw pure bare & bare raw pure
is a blue and black cliff
a train crosses the forest

it's raining upon man of many names
alone and unselved   daydreamer
who vaguely vapes
in the ordinary tumult
the wind poor polyvalent paving stone
tumbles and skids left and right
throws in his face
packets of leaves
(maple chestnut
alder and dogwood)
and twittering birds
(blackbirds tits
 warblers and chaffinches)

and here he is grinding
his bones into all
available means exclaiming "Yes *tempus alas fugit
inreparabile* and *fugaces labuntur anni* but
the sea remains
              and at least
let the embrace go on she
who softly binds and unbinds me
so that eternity shall yet be
at last and always
              still young"

March 17, 2018

Pluie vent vitesse

Le ciel à contre-emploi
cru pur nu   nu cru pur   & pur nu cru
est une falaise bleue et noire
un train traverse la forêt

il pleut sur l'homme au cent noms
seul et sans soi   rêvasseur
qui vaguement vapote
dans l'ordinaire tumulte
le vent pavé triste polyvalent
tourneboule et débarde à tout va
lui jette au visage
paquets de feuillages
(érables châtaigniers
aulnes et cornouillers)
et d'oiseaux piaillants
(merles mésanges
fauvettes et pinsons)

et voilà qu'il mouline
ses os fait flèche
de tout bois s'exclame «Oui *tempus eheu fugit
inreparabile* et *fugaces labuntur anni* mais
il reste la mer
    et qu'encore
au moins m'enlace celle
qui doucement me lie me délie
pour que l'éternité soit encore
enfin toujours
    encore jeune »

17 mars 2018

Bulletin (supplement)

The wind imperfect the breeze profuse fry
sweeps golden acres   crosses and un-
crosses the quickened flows
formidably rhythmic
then wearily ravages and dismantles
the hirsute Hercynian herbage
the guingettes lamps
limpets and trinkets aslant

it's half
lit vermillion ingot
the hazy light so soon to fade and die
in the thick and porous shadow
of the undergrowth

inevitable the clouds
(cartilage wool & crepe)
barbed wire bearded approach
unroll their frilliness
their fiercely free story
figureless plotless and without
beginning nor anything
that does not end

(...*to be continued*)

March 22, 2018

Bulletin (supplément)

Le vent plus qu'imparfait la brise drue friture
balaie des arpents d'or   croise et dé-
croise les flots précipités
rythmiques formidablement
puis ravage lasse et démantèle
l'hirsute hercynienne herbe
les guinguettes quinquets
breloques de guingois et berniques

c'est le demi
jour lingot vermillon
l'indécise clarté déjà qui s'exténue
dans l'ombre perméable épaisse
d'un sous-bois

les inévitables les nuages
(cartilages ouate & papier crépon)
barbelés barbus s'avancent
déroulent leurs fanfreluches
leur histoire farouchement libre sans
figures sans intrigues ni
commencement ni rien
qui ne finit pas

(...*à suivre*)

22 mars 2018

Continuation

acid is the suint of the pack
windy wooly pot-bellied
gas muzzles brays squawks
spouts steelworks' racket   fires
—*white/ red/ green*—
beacons and squalls
the flows' chaos balances out
the one-legged Arthur is hauled aboard

it's the slack dawn
                grace at last
the sullen swell at the bitter end
the cold water where glimmers scatter
already dead
stars my taciturn beauties
the inevitable delicious clouds
(bundles of cartilage wool & crepe)
the greenish and leaden sun
which a storm streaks with purples heaving to

the hermaphroditic centauries
the fork pale and bald of a eucalyptus
the inevitable rooks chirp
kwaakwaakwaak
in the flowering chestnuts
black copses against the red sky

Continuation

acide est le suint de la meute
ventue velue ventrue
gaz mufles ébrais rauquements
trombes vacarme d'aciérie   feux
—*blancs/ rouges/ verts*—
balises et bourrasques
le désordre des flux s'équilibre
on hisse à bord l'unijambiste Arthur

c'est l'aube étale
                la grâce enfin
la houle morne au bout du rouleau
l'eau froide où se dispersent
les lueurs mortes déjà
des étoiles mes belles taciturnes
les inévitables délicieux nuages
(fagots de cartilage ouate & papier crépon)
le soleil verdâtre et plombé
que violace un orage à la cape

les centaurées hermaphrodites
la fourche pâle et glabre d'un eucalyptus
les freux immanquables craquettent
kwaakwaakwaak
dans les marronniers en fleur
taillis noirs sur le ciel rouge

you'll say that the words sp(l)it us
by rare chance
tell me do you
recall you little soul
cuddlesome animule blandula
eternal virgule and teeny-weeny blessed
pile of it all

May 5, 2018

on dira que les mots nous c(r)achent
au rare ha-
sard dis t'en
resouviens-tu petite âme
câline animule blandule
éternelle virgule et tout petit béni
tas de tout

5 mai 2018

Nothing (a whole lot of)

far off in a peripheral county of the universes
an emerald lightning bolt in a nanosecond
simulacrum of a hurricane inexorable and devastating
fluid explosive hedgehog
and pointed hunchbacked boxy
pulverizes crumbles a galaxy

the day yes the day
to day here washed up
grey yellow rag
iron corridor
parlor for rincing with soot/ tin/ pitch
drawer full of compost and black bones

flavorless the polyvalent sky
without lightning fire wind
(you can hear *pschhh*)
that anger it shake it up
that sift it

the ruckus of the sea
vat of dreams abyss
omnivore grinning and bearing it whirlpools
that a ferry prunes off

a harrow hairy and fossilized loses its teeth
at the edge of the wide far off in back
of the downward side through
the heights of the bottom (left)
of a freshly plowed field

Rien (trois fois)

très loin dans un canton périphérique des univers
un éclair émeraude d'une nanoseconde
simulacre d'ouragan inexorable et dévastant
hérisson fluide explosif
et pointu bossu boxu
pulvérise émiette une galaxie

le jour oui l'au
jour le jour ici lessivé
haillon gris jaune
couloir de fonte
parloir à rinçures à suie/ étain/ brai
tiroir chargé de compost et d'os noirs

fade le ciel polyvalent
sans les foudres le feu les vents
(on entend *pschhh*)
qui l'encolèrent le secouent
le blutent

le vacarme de la mer
baquet des rêves gouffre
omnivore au dos rond tourbillons
qu'un ferry taille sec

une herse hirsute et fossilisée s'édente
au bord du long loin derrière
le côté d'en bas à travers
la hauteur du fond (à gauche)
d'un labour frais

somewhere someone a bud
a bauble a herald
with tubas and blunderbusses
while there's still time
yet persists
(impatience hazy and splendid)
aligns disarticulates
two words or forty-
seven or two-hundred thirty-eight

jabbering fidgeting
the lyre and all the tralala
boom boom with feeling
ah just make us laugh

in a blue forest the dream
is darnel nettle sea holly in fistfulls
a sheet you make holes in

far from the city
the moon creaks
and starts to glow again
in the clouds wool and suint
felts lovely and fruit-bearing

only afterwards do we start again
looking for a wall

July 5, 2018

quelque part quelqu'un bourgeon
brimborion chantre
à tubas et tromblons
pendant qu'il en est temps
encore s'entête
(impatience confuse et splendide)
aligne désarticule
deux mots ou quarante-
sept ou deux cent trente-huit

baragouins et remuements
toute la lyre et rantanplans
des boums boums et du sentiment
ah dis donc fais nous rire

dans une forêt bleue le rêve
c'est l'ivraie l'ortie le panicaut qu'on empoigne
un drap qu'on troue

loin de la ville
la lune grince
et recommence à luire
dans les nuages laines et suints
feutres beaux et fruitiers

après seulement on recommence
on cherche un mur

5 juillet 2018

Frivolities

the wee bare creek
gets muddled and mixed up
in the vast inevitable river
farther off behind the blue trees
hurried empties itself into the abyss the blackness
Erebus where furtive and tarred
live the devouring
hideous blind beasts

sky broken grafted
high cloud stirred square which
   —clandestine—
slipper or ballast
chaffed ragpicking
wool with suint
               presses on
in the entropic hook
the golden pickaxe the lightning

bursting original soup-pot
older than any shadow   the sea
hunchbacked hedgehog mold
for dreams for whirlpools
lacuna all of a sud
den   shrieking vertigo   stupendously
open mouth in which to feed annoyance
spunk boiling dribbling beating
the little cliff and the dike
the unending of winters at long last

Frivolités

le menu nu ruisseau
s'emmêle et mêle
au vaste inévitable fleuve
plus loin derrière les arbres bleus
précipité se dépote à l'abîme au noir
Erèbe où furtives bitumeuses
se tiennent les dévorantes
hideuses aveugles bêtes

ciel cassé bouturé
haut nuage brassé carré qui
   —clandestin—
pantoufle ou ballast
chiffonnerie raguée
laine à suints
           s'opiniâtre
dans l'entropique accroc
la pioche d'or la foudre

détonante soupière originelle
plus vieille que toute ombre   la mer
hérisson bossu moule
à songes à tourbillons
lacune tout-à-
coup   hurlant vertige   ahuri
bâîllement où nourrir l'ennui
foutre qui bout bave et bat
la petite falaise et la digue
l'incessé des hivers à la fin

to regret and regret the greenery
the frostbite the freezing
cinder coaldust the fertile earth
the bramble the purple love grass the darnel
the violet
         one enters
without fanfare neither crowned
nor frightened lawless
flowerless without reproach
flameless heartless
soundless
             in the enormous unheard-of
             what what
             what?
and all this like
a fluid rustling a shiver
a searing crackle
neutral barely which
would be only would be
meaning supposedly

in the season of the strongest
the soul is always farthest

October 3, 2018

au regret au regret les verdures
les onglées les gelures
cendre poussier la terre féconde
la ronce l'herbe d'amour l'ivraie
la violette
        on entre
sans tambours ni couronnes
ni peur sans loi ni
fleurs reproches sans
feu lieu
ni trompettes
            dans l'énorme inouï
            quoi quoi
            quoi?
et tout ça comme
un bruissement fluide un frisson
un crépitement fulgurant
neutre à peine qui ne
serait que serait
censément le sens

la saison du plus mort
c'est toujours l'âme ailleurs

3 octobre 2018

The Depths of Time

December wreckage umbrage flayed
Adolphe Thiers Street
(French politician 1797-1877)
the lampposts spit crude and fine
their gold
it is ten to six I asked you for the time
that's not the real subject

Charettes Road:
- *What does your father do?*
- *What does yours do?*
  What does your mother do?

Écoute-s'il-pleut Way:
- *I don't like chemistry.*
- *My dog's name is Arthur.*
  "The birds fly away and the flowers fall"
  there's no better title.
- *Yes there is.*

Révolution Square:
- *No one is serious*
- *At 17.*

Albert Mahieu Street
- *I'll be a ship's steward.*
- *I'll be an actuary or a scenographer*
or nothing

Le fonds des temps

Décembre décembre ombre écorchée
rue Adolphe Thiers
(homme politique français 1797-1877)
les lampadaires crachent cru menu
leur or
il est 18h moins 10 je t'ai demandé l'heure
ça n'est pas le sujet réel

rue des Charettes:
- *Que fait ton père?*
- *Que fait le tien?*
  Que fait ta mère?

passage de l'Écoute-s'il-pleut:
- *Je n'aime pas la chimie.*
- *Mon chien s'appelle Arthur.*
  «Les oiseaux s'envolent et les fleurs tombent»
  il n'est pas de titre plus beau.
- *Si.*

place de la Révolution:
- *On n'est pas sérieux*
- *On a 17 ans.*

rue Albert Mahieu
- *Je serai commissaire de marine.*
- *Je serai actuaire ou scénographe*
  ou rien

Henri Gréville Square seven o'clock:
- *see you tomorrow.*

Square sky.
        Solitude.

November 4, 2018

place Henri Gréville dix-neuf heures:
- *à demain.*

Ciel carré.
         Solitude.

4 novembre 2018

Destocking

nothing more than black jackets
of tarry oakum drifting
and on the fly these are the carping
curt and hoarse *kroa kraa* crows

a pigeon rows across the patched-up sky
great cloudiness fuchsia mauve
turquoise where dispossessed contingent man
the investigator distractedly eyes and counts
Saturn's chaos and eternities
lost milkiness the galaxies
some polychrome lumps
lightning in his eyes   scrap   sperm-whale memory

    ***

(Episode)

drunken stuttering asthmatic puppet
the disheveled moldering sybil full of fancy
limps and lows:

«Ibant obscuri sola sub nocte
the hunters striving advancing
in the open the opaque
transparency of shadow
and their rending dogs
blue meat raw meat
they bark to debone

Déstockage

plus que noires jaquettes
d'étoupe bitumeuse à la dérive
et vanvole ce sont à grincher
sec et rauque *kroa kraa* les corneilles

un pigeon rame au ciel rapiécé
grand nuagier fuchsia mauve
turquoise où dépossédé éventuel l'homme
l'investigateur distraitement lorgne et décompte
le chaos de Saturne et les éternités
laitances égarées les galaxies
quelques grumeaux polychromes
foudre aux yeux   ferraille   cachalot-mémoire

***

(Episode)

fantoche ivre bègue asthmatique
l'échevelée fabulante avariée la sybille
claudique et mugit:

«Ibant obscuri sola sub nocte
les chasseurs s'efforçant avançant
dans l'ouvert et l'opaque
transparence de l'ombre
et leurs déchirants chiens
viande bleue viande crue
ça aboie pour désosser

the one who meanwhile scampers
furry hairy fuguing vainly
(he knows it) in the hasty
night the broken wind   the little
snow to laugh at
               and the muck
heart withdrawn in the cold blue
crumpled undeniable
and beneath the shorn pockmarked knobbed orb
the moon numb in the swirls
there he is by his cresped mane
clung to hooked on the tree sinister black
wriggling dangling
still-life and stilled
               life »

the dogs are coming...

       ***

                      ...and the perfect wind
the happy slap of a downpour upon the abyss
the red hills and the heath...

November 5, 2018

celui qui cependant décampe
velu chevelu vainement fugard
(il le sait) dans la nuit
précipitée le vent rompu   la petite
neige à rire
    et la poisse
coeur dessaisi dans le bleu froid
froissé indiscutable
et sous l'astre grêlé tondu bossu
la lune engourdie dans les tourbillons
le voilà par son crin crippu
agrippé croché dans l'arbre glauque noir
gigotant pendouillant
nature morte et mort
    subite »

les chiens arrivent...

   ***

     ... et le vent parfait
la claque heureuse d'une averse sur l'abîme
les collines rouges et la lande...

5 novembre 2018

Ancient History 1

To start with you put
all the cows in the same manger
and the dead—having crossed the measly black river—
are on the island   silent
lost in the swamps
the muck the peatbog
they are waiting

        then

planting in the old blind waves the shovels
pulling hard
      or broad reach put out to sea
hauling the sheets
sailing to the island embarking
yonder   to
    shut up
COME ON YOU MUMUSES!
knowing at long last
this modest and complicated art
of firmly holding your tongue
    to stay alive

November 26, 2018

Histoire Ancienne 1

Pour commencer on met
tous les boeufs dans le même casier
et les morts—passé le fleuve piètre et noir—
sont dans l'île   taiseux
perdus dans les paluds
les fanges la tourbière
ils attendent

        alors

planter aux vieux aveugles flots les pelles
souquer
       ou grand largue mettre à la voile
embraquer les écoutes
courir à l'île s'embarquer
pour là-bas   pour
    s'y taire
ASSEZ LES MUMUSES!
connaître à la longue
cet art modeste & compliqué
tenir fermement sa langue
   rester vivants

26 novembre 2018

Ancient History 2

Wild lovely strange prescription
for a better sojourn:
very little
the buzzard stunned
curlews lapwings turnstones
somewhere in a night to come
a nightjar purrs and chortles
daffodils jasmine
the eagle fern unfurling its crosiers
from one bank to the other on the naked water
the flexible ricochet of an echo
—*echo of whom echo of what?*—
the snow that stutters
on a line of blue shingles
the rushing wind that gangles
twirling
and up there over there   breaks the soul
Boötes Centaurus Arcturus and Virgo
and everything *shall be what it is no longer* or *was what it shall be*

It's a narrow escape

November 26, 2018

Histoire Ancienne 2

Sauvage belle étrange ordonnance
pour un séjour meilleur:
peu de choses
la buse variable éberluée
courlis vanneaux tournepierres
quelque part dans une nuit à venir
un engoulevent ronronne et glousse
jonquilles jasmins
la fougère aigle qui déplie ses crosses
d'une rive à l'autre sur l'eau nue
le ricochet flexible d'un écho
—écho de qui écho de quoi?—
la neige qui bégaie
sur un cordon de galets bleus
le vent rué qui dégingande
à la virevolte
et là-haut là-bas   brise l'âme
le Bouvier le Centaure Arcturus et la Vierge
et tout *sera ce qu'il n'est plus* ou *fut ce qu'il sera*

C'est l'échappée belle

26 novembre 2018

Sketch

Obtuse pathetic stuttering
I am says the erstwhile mortal *I am*
more or less
        here
beneath the sky unwrapped wan
congested —clouds on the loose
        grey light—
where the wind works
in broad swathes

and nothing except
a cat poaching and the shower
on the sea at no reasonable
hour substantial harrowing

the night like an axe
then the sun enraged red and coming out
of the opposing woods

it's going to rain
someone is going to speak shout
in the brush

December 17, 2018

Esquisse

Obtus piètre bègue
je suis dit le ci-devant mortel *je suis*
à peu près
        là
sous le ciel déballé blafard
obstrué   —nuages buissonniers
        lumière grise—
où le vent travaille
dans les grandes largeurs

et rien sinon
un chat qui braconne et l'ondée
sur la mer à pas
d'heure   hersée substantielle

la nuit comme une hache
puis le soleil enragé rouge et qui sort
du bois d'en face

il va pleuvoir
quelqu'un va parler tonner
dans la broussaille

17 décembre 2018

Memorandum

The wind upright tumbled down
faster than fast
from the perfect north
plows lugs dishevels
the reddish grass the little
blonde & wild oats
where the acridians are encased

what remains of *cloudy vapors*
shrouds of soot shrouds of silk
comes undone over the marly black scree
the Hercynian lividities of rocks
muffled by cornflowers by thistles
by rosebuds

a flock of starlings twists and turns
the sea pronounces its grunt and rant

what goes on too long it too much goes

January 6, 2019

Pour Mémoire

Le vent crispé dévalé
à qui mieux mieux
depuis le nord parfait
charrue charrie dépeigne
les herbes rousses les petites
avoines sauvages & blondes
où s'encaquent les acridiens

ce qui reste de *vapeurs nuagières*
suaires à suies suaires à soies
se défait sur l'éboulis marneux noir
les lividités hercyniennes des rocs
feutrés de bleuets de chardons
de roses en bouton

un vol d'étourneaux tourneboule et vire
la mer fait son grommelot/coup de gueule

va trop qui trop dure

6 janvier 2019

Juxtapositions

man is this living thing
—more and more mortal—
saturated with vague shadows
of ulterior immemorable dreams
of sublime emotions although
possibly always superficial
of sentimental excesses and melancholies
vertigo desire weariness passion
irresistable inexhaustible turbulent
etc... etc...
and sometimes in the low sublunary world
at the hazy edges of a garden of delights
(May roses carnivorous titmice)
he speaks to his invisible brothers

the nightjar has fallen silent
the fox has not yelped
forests grow misty where bell
discreetly wild beasts
a lazy rain percolates through copses
and the rigorously black yews
the wind grows irate and jags
the sea my sweetheart is here
not just a little and the armadas
have sunk low—the abyss
        teaches nothing

January 27, 2019

Juxtapositions

l'homme est ce vivant
—mortel de plus en plus—
saturé d'ombres vagues
d'ultérieurs immémorables rêves
d'émotions sublimes quoique
possiblement toujours superficielles
de désordres sentimentaux et mélancolies
vertiges désirs lassitudes passions
irrésistibles inépuisables turbulentes
etc... etc...
et quelquefois dans le bas monde sublunaire
aux lisières confuses d'un jardin des délices
(roses de mai mésanges carnivores)
il parle à ses frères invisibles

l'engoulevent s'est tu
le renard n'a pas glapi
des forêts s'embuent où brament
des bêtes discrètement sauvages
une pluie paresseuse percole des taillis
et les ifs rigoureusement noirs
le vent s'énerve et déchire
la mer ma mignonne est là
pas qu'un peu et les armadas
coulées bas—l'abîme
        n'enseigne rien

27 janvier 2019

Oompahs

A sad gale unstitches shakes
the sky inevitably
and the sea where you dream of your love
faraway *and little lamzy divey*

(*we're being jerked off* someone says)

it rains shadow and man
voracious insatiable machine
of desire is at his
hallucinatory maundering
upon the hairy manger
in slate offshore
he dreams

      afterward you know no longer
the sky was a chewed dug up marvel
in a clearing   the good weather
returning blazes at the coast
the gold layered bristling delightful
the tousled chaos
of the gorse   of the burning orpin
a little plover as calm
as can be
pecks at the bank
the gentler wind blows again
wherever it wants
      sour bugle melan
cholic in a minor key
the shepherdess your love
faraway *mairzy doats* faraway *dozy doats*
runs off —we are long ago— her sheeps and goats
she never tires

February 10, 2019

Flonflons

Une bourrasque triste découd secoue
le ciel immanquablement
et la mer où l'on rêve à l'aimée
lointaine *mironton mironton mirontaine*

(*on se fait branler* dit quelqu'un)

il pleut de l'ombre et l'homme
vorace insatiable machine
à désirs est à sa
bourlingue hallucinée
sur la mangeoire hirsute
ardoisière hauturière
il rêve

      après on ne sait plus
le ciel était mâchée bêchée merveille
par une éclaircie   le grand beau
revenu flambe à la côte
l'or échelonné hérissé jouissif
le désordre ébouriffé
de l'ajonc   de l'orpin brûlant
un petit gravelot le plus
tranquillement du monde
picotte à la grève
le vent radouci resouffle
où il veut
      aigre cornet mélan
colique en mineur
la bergère l'aimée
lointaine *tonton* lointaine *tontaine*
file —on est jadis— son coton ses laines
inlassablement

10 février 2019

Twilight

wandering hazy and feigned
triplets in daydreams   words
wordless and without
music echo
of irremediable death small
medium and large

the whole lyre in the common district
the sullen pleasure
the exuberant velocity the detours
unexpected the enflamed confusion
in the sky by billhook shredded cubed
chewed
the far off opacity of twilight

and me? what did you think?
says someone
now I uninhabit
here there far off beyond…

February 25, 2019

CRÉPUSCULE

Errance indécise et feinte
triolets rêveurs   paroles
sans paroles
ni musique écho
de l'irrémédiable mort petite
moyenne et grande

toute la lyre au commun canton
le plaisir morne
l'exubérante vélocité les détours
inattendus l'embrasement confus
au ciel à la serpe écharpé maçonné
mâchouillé
l'opacité lointaine du crépuscule

et moi? qu'avez-vous cru?
dit quelqu'un
*désormais j'inhabite
ici là là-bas ailleurs...*

25 février 2019

Discharge

1

night of cockayne
the great bellows the shaky
wind jostles and displaces
the gentle pitch of the cumulo
nimbus the cabin far off on the dune

2

the sea lullaby patient and hairy
bludgeons the steep cliff
scrams and decamps
at dock and quay number 22
    at the bumped dike
the sky is thickness is a bird
torn in the tree it's
a cloud barley and rye
it passes by

3

men have grown silent
and whitened their hands
they sharpen their blades
divide the hanged men's noose
taste the black weeds
drink tankards of bitter cider
recognize the raw scent of mares
never do they listen to the blind
never do they look at the deaf
and they disenchant: *"Here is sunday*

Quitus

1

nuit de cocagne
le grand soufflet le vent
tremblé bouscule et déménage
le roulis doux des cumulo
nimbus la cabane au loin sur la dune

2

la mer berceuse patiente chevelue
matraque la falaise accore
décanille et décampe
au dock au quai numéro 22
      à la digue emboutie
le ciel c'est de l'épais c'est un oiseau
déchiré dans l'arbre c'est
un nuage orge et seigle
ça passe

3

les hommes ont fait silence
et blanchi leurs mains
ils affûtent leurs lames
partagent la corde des pendus
goûtent l'herbe noire
boivent au broc du cidre amer
reconnaissent l'odeur crue des juments
jamais ils n'écoutent les aveugles
ils ne regardent pas les sourds
et déchantent: «*Voilà dimanche*

deboned ransacked man is
to fall into spare parts
from the savage cloud
flesh of the trough and the cupboard
meat for coffins
meat for God
that's soon to be us."

    4

the jays fly low
the dogs cross the soilless ageless
forest of omens and dreams
a horse laughs near a pump
a mirror pool almost blue and dried up sediments
the intersected reaches flare up
into the river the bundles are thrown
the firebugs *pyrrhocoris apterus*
with their red and black chevrons teem in a flowerbed
the liners glide off the islets

    5

it is a bit past 8pm UTC
and the perpetual dreamer Tom Thumb in his wandering
opens very wide his blue little eyes
peeps and sputters mutters
his thanksgiving

March 19, 2019

> *désossé saccagé l'homme est*
> *à choir en pièces détachées*
> *de la nue sauvage*
> *chair d'auge et d'armoire*
> *bidoche à cercueil*
> *bidoche à Dieu*
> *c'est bientôt nous* ».

4

les geais filent bas
les chiens traversent la forêt hors sol
hors temps des présages et des songes
un cheval rit près d'une pompe
un étang miroir presque bleu tari sédimente
les biefs intersectés flamboient
à la rivière les fagots sont jetés
les gendarmes *pyrrhocoris apterus*
aux chevrons rouges et noirs grouillent dans un parterre
les paquebots glissent au large des îlots

5

il est 20h et des poussières T.U.
et le sempiternel poucet rêveur à sa vadrouille
ouvre très grand ses petits bleus yeux
zyeute et balbutie marmonne
son action de grâce

19 mars 2019

Chivaree, certified true copy.

Gawker loitering and quiet
distraught and itching with
weariness and melancholy
he speaks of something else to the four corners
of the fabulous world
abolished unpolished populated
with uncertain anticipation
the timeout gnaws
his flesh raw (and your own)
and his hands stretched over the little fire

the drizzle dissipates inevitably
over a frolicsome dog practically blue
the abrupt open coppice where lovers love each other
a split cauldron among the fireweed
the osmunda and the foxgloves
the wallow down below where the hogs grovel
a trawler fishing out to sea
the anvil of a cape flowered with heath
that dusk cancels out

the well-groomed sky at fault
and faulted piles up
the wind hors d'âge pulls up weeds
what is seen is the shadow
a woman passing then another and then
still another and children
who will soon be all of ash and dust
in the great whole the great hole
the Great Hole there there too
and time sledgehammers

Charivari, p.c.c.

Badaud musard et coi
que les lassitudes et la mélancolie
démangent et désemparent
il parle d'autre chose aux quatre coins
du fabuleux monde
aboli dépoli peuplé
d'attentes incertaines
le temps mort mord à vif
sa viande (et la vôtre)
et ses mains à tendre au petit feu

la bruine se dissipe inévitablement
sur un chien jouasse et quasi bleu
le taillis abrupt ouvert où les amants s'aiment
un chaudron fendu parmi les épilobes
l'osmonde et les digitales
la bauge par en-bas où se vautrent les porcs
un chalutier en pêche au large
l'enclume d'un cap à lande fleurie
que le crépuscule oblitère

le ciel débarbouillé coupable
découpable s'entasse
le vent hors d'âge désherbe
ce que l'on voit c'est l'ombre
une femme qui passe puis une autre et puis
une autre encore et des enfants
qui bientôt seront tretous cendre et poudre
au grand tout le grand trou
le Grand Trou là là itou
et le temps marteau-pilonne

Farewell lovely days black and pink
farewell living creatures fair
farewell words on which I think
farewell windy air
farewell its humming just before
eternity neither
paralyzed nor decalcomaniacal

April 20, 2019

Adieu les beaux jours noirs et roses
adieu les vivants
adieu les morts auxquels je cause
adieu le vent
adieu son ronron juste
avant l'éternité ni paralysée ni
décalcomaniaque.

20 avril 2019

Good And Grand

The hail *tacatac   tchac*
shot up the barley the opaque pond
the place called *of the lost hanged wolf*
a grey field where crows dive
and dismantle
the dreaded stag beetle
with extravagant mandibles
all the good and grand disorder
of the centauries lady's bedstraw catchweed
vain ornaments   natural prehistory
and all the bygone sky absent scalloped
wideopen
rag and bramble misreckoning and gash

a barren dries upon the cliff
the streams steam in yon
der pastures old as
paths at night the wind
wild and the sea
with its spring tides unsymetrical
interim

imminent
bursting out in the unrincing yaw
of shadow and the retreat
of a cloud chipped unstitched
floats the semblance of a black
smile whose grace all of a sudden
boisters
        then more
                or less is erased

Grand Beau

La grêle *tacatac   tchac*
a mitraillé les orges l'opaque étang
le lieu-dit *du loup perdu pendu*
un pré gris où les corbeaux s'abattent
et démantèlent
la redoutable lucane
aux extravagants mandibules
tout le grand beau désordre
des centaurées caille-lait gratterons
vains ornements   préhistoire naturelle
et tout le jadis ciel absent échancré
grantouvert
guenille et roncier mécompte et déchirure

un sécheron sèche sur la falaise
les eaux fument dans les eaux-
delà d'herbages vieux comme
les chemins la nuit le vent
sauvage et la mer
aux vives-eaux dissymétriques
intérimaires

imminent
surgi dans les dérinçures un embardement
d'ombre et le repli
d'un nuage ébréché décousu
flotte un semblant de sourire
noir dont la grâce tout-à-coup
désopile
        puis plus
                ou moins s'efface

here the imperfect frees
and God is the little scribbling child
astray nailed up

May 11, 2019

ici l'imparfait délivre
et Dieu c'est le petit enfant scribouilleur
et perdu cloué

11 mai 2019

Parade

The sea's a meadow won back
field of shells & encrusted placenta
dowser   sooty wretched mirror
straw bed for buddies and mess tin of stars
the immense sizzling memorial gravedigger
cauldron of metaphors and road
in the open
for sharing and in destitution for labor
despite the knowledge always uncertain
it ripens vaguely among the grain
the drizzles the dreams
                    to go on

deep in an enclosure a blue man
kneads his face and weeps
cackles chuckles and weeps

Profuse(ly) the wind stays out
rolls in the isle *of many promises*
the rosehip the milkweed
the samphire and the watercress
a poplar grows green
the dawn confused and milky
is.

May 30, 2019

Parade

La mer c'est pré gagné
champ d'écailles & placenta croustillé
sourcier   fulgurant misérable miroir
paillasse à compagnons et gamelle aux étoiles
l'énorme crépitant fossoyeur mémoriel
chaudron des métaphores et route
dans l'ouvert
pour le partage et le dénuement la besogne
malgré les toujours incertains savoirs
ça mûrit vaguement dans les grains
les bruines les songes
                    pour aller

au fond d'un enclos un homme bleu
se laboure et pleure
ricane rigole et pleure

Le vent épais(sement) découche
roule dans l'île *aux cent promesses*
le gratte-cul le laiteron
la salicorne et le cresson
un peuplier verdit
l'aube confuse et laiteuse
c'est.

30 mai 2019

Downtime

the wind blew somewhere
from the yellow sky the cumulo-
nimbus *soot   pale horde*
throw down their giant shadows
the vertigo is a promise
(or the reverse)

"let's go my pussy cat
in Kithyra we'll tarry
who's that, ratatat-tat
off to the cemetery"

the undulating salamanders
diverse surreptitious
clip the waters slit the silt
the half-light in the cool moats
of the dark forbidden castle
dresser full of peelings   smashed
*—the yokels saw it
assailed it then destroyed it—*
some rats whine
a dog limps
in a pasture some cows degas
the flow-flowing water
bathes the alder grove nearby

Temps Mort

le vent a sifflé quelque part
du ciel jaune les cumulo-
nimbus *suies   pâle horde*
jettent à bas leurs ombres géantes
le vertige est promesse
(ou l'inverse)

«allons-nous / lons-nous en
voulez-vous aux Cythères
et viens t'en rantanplan
z'aux cimetières »

les ondulantes salamandres
diverses subreptices
fendent les eaux les limons
la pénombre aux douves fraîches
du château obscur interdit
armoire d'épluchures   mis à bas
—*les croquants le virent*
l'assaillirent puis le détruisirent—
des rats gémissent
un chien boite
dans un herbage des vaches dégazent
l'eau coulant-coulante
baigne tout près l'aulnaie

rainy days
soon a tense light
the last winter
toes in the water toes in the grass
pumps full of straw
and bruised apples
the snow is set free
chilling peeling
nipping chapping
patching dispatching
the night rethickens
each promise here is vertigo
(or the reverse)

June 8, 2019

jours à pluies
bientôt lumière crispée
le dernier hiver
les pieds dans l'eau les pieds dans l'herbe
pompes empaillées
et pommes gaulées
la neige se délivre
froidure pelure
gerçure gelure
perlure rature
la nuit reprend son épaisseur
toute promesse est ici vertige
(ou l'inverse)

8 juin 2019

Impromptu

under the wind in the west
the rough draft   dairy and bakery
of the morning mist
in the delicious surly skinny sky
a choppy breeze that vitrifies
the light impoverished modest
and a little later that cloud there
substantial urban almost
square black and crested fringed
with a frothy tuft

the tiny trotting of **real** fieldmice
all this   rubble vain
ornaments bony underbrushed
bits of junk and barrels

shepherds hunters little
children Tims tiny tiny
and patient just enough
to make memory
—time enough for a dream out of joint—
in sleepage and sleepery

the unabating the groping
the stamping the restlessness pell-mell
and colic abandon
into the opaque to
advance march erase oneself in
the twilight softness
refuge yet to nothing refuge
    to loss
      imperceptibly

July 7, 2019

Impromptu

sous le vent dans l'ouest
le brouillon   laitages et boulanges
du ciel délicieux bourru maigre
des brumes matinales
une brise hachée vitrifie
la lumière appauvrie modeste
et peu après le nuage là-bas
substantiel urbain presque
carré noir et crêté
d'une floche écumeuse

le trot menu des mulots **réels**
tout ça   décombres vains
ornements ossus broussaillus
rogatons et fûtailles

bergers chasseurs petits
enfants poucets petits petits
et patients juste assez
pour faire mémoire
—le temps disjoint d'un songe—
dans le dormage et la dormure

l'acharnement l'à tâtons
la piaffe et la hâte mais
l'*encoliquement* l'abandon
à l'opaque pour
avancer marcher s'effacer dans
la douceur crépusculaire
refuge au pourtant rien refuge
      au manque
         insaisissablement

7 juillet 2019

Acknowledgments

The original French poems of *Showers and Bright Spells* are mostly drawn from four of Henri Droguet's collections: *Maintenant ou jamais* (Belin, 2013), *Désordre du jour* (Gallimard, 2016), *Palimpsestes et Rigodons* (Potentille, 2016), and *Grandeur nature* (Rehauts, 2020).

Clatters first appeared as a chapbook edition from Ohm Press / Rain Taxi in 2015. Some of the "bonus poems" were published online by Rain Taxi to accompany this chapbook. *Clatters* is the translation of the original chapbook *Boucans* published by Wigwam in 2010. Two poems from *Clatters*, "Soliloquy" and "Literally," have appeared in *The Colorado Review*. A few French original versions from the Bonus Poems included in *Clatters* also appeared in Henri Droguet's *Maintenant ou jamais* (Editions Belin, 2013).

"Quatuor no. 3" and "Ritornello" first appeared in *Literary Imagination*. "In the Ancient Manner," "Update," "Artist's Trial," "Brief," "Bulletin (supplement)," "Continuation," "Nothing (a Whole Lot Of)," "Frivolities," "The Depths of Time," "Destocking," and "Ancient History" first appeared in *Trafika Europe*, no. 18.

Some of these poems and translations were read at the University of Chicago in Paris' French and American Poetry Symposium on March 23, 2017. Thanks to Rosanna Warren for her generous support in organizing this event.

The translator would like to thank Henri Droguet for his constant friendship for nearly twenty years, and for his indispensable assistance and collaboration on the present translations.

HENRI DROGUET was born in 1944 in Cherbourg, Normandy. He studied history and literature at the University of Caen. Until 2004, he taught literature in Saint-Malo, where he has lived since 1972. He has published some dozen collections of poetry, most with Gallimard; the latest, *Grandeur nature*, was published by Rehauts. He has also published two books of prose; the most recent, with Fario Editions, is called *Faisez pas les cons!* When he is not reading, he writes; when he is not writing, he gardens, he wanders, he runs to the opera house, he sails from Saint-Malo to Lorient, or else out toward English Cornwall, the Scillies, Ireland.

ALEXANDER DICKOW was born in Lexington, Kentucky, and grew up in Moscow, Idaho. He is associate professor of French at Virginia Tech, and a novelist, translator, scholar and poet who writes in French and English. His latest book is *Le Premier Souper*, a novel published by La Volte in 2021. Forthcoming translations include works by Sylvie Kandé and Max Jacob.